# The Ultimate Beginner Guide to Blowing Up on YouTube in 2019

How to Use Social Media Marketing and Facebook Advertising to Become an Influencer and Build the Business of Your Dreams

*Written by Bennie Sloan*

purposes only. All effort has been executed to present accurate, up to date, and reliable, complete information. No warranties of any kind are declared or implied. Readers acknowledge that the author is not engaging in the rendering of legal, financial, medical or professional advice. The content within this book has been derived from various sources. Please consult a licensed professional before attempting any techniques outlined in this book.

By reading this document, the reader agrees that under no circumstances is the author responsible for any losses, direct or indirect, which are incurred as a result of the use of information contained within this document, including, but not limited to, — errors, omissions, or inaccuracies.

# Table of Contents

# Introduction

Welcome to a new era of internet business and digital media. It is a world where you can learn anything and do anything. It is a new world of value, passion, and creativity—a world where you can make revenue doing what you like doing.

Thanks to YouTube and other social media outlets, every one of us can rise and broadcast how we view life to a global audience. For once, people can access a similar audience which was usually only for core television networks and those wealthy enough to advertise.

However, this does not imply that just anybody can pick up a video camera, make a video and gain exposure automatically. No, there are steps to it. However, every one of us can create our special corner on YouTube to develop an audience of following for our perspective.

Irrespective of the kind of message you plan on spreading on YouTube, in your hands lies the power to impact a large number of people using video on demand. Even the largest stars have their own YouTube space. However, the question on the lips of many individuals is this; is it possible to earn revenue from YouTube? Well, in short, the answer is YES. But it is still dependent on what you define as earning income.

But, you have to also know that social media is not the same as it was 2 years back. The strategies which worked in 2016 or 2017 are already obsolete and won't work in 2019. That is why I have written this book. It contains all the fresh strategies that would be useful to you this year and would help you be on your way to earning the revenue you desire.

In the chapters to come, you will be learning how to make all of this possible. You will find out how to develop a presence on YouTube, how to find your niche, How to make great videos among many others.

Then, when you have uploaded your videos, you

will also learn how you can distribute and promote them so it won't get lost in the barrage of videos viewers add to the website daily.

A whole lot of others have succeeded in making their dreams on YouTube a reality and others have failed. So why were some successful and why did others fail? Well, we will be covering all of that in this book.

I do not promise that there won't be any hassles or you won't run into problems on the way. Being a YouTuber comes with its issues. But, I assure you that when you are through reading this book, you will have a comprehensive knowledge of being a YouTuber. Also, if you do use all of the information this book provides, you will be able to run your channel and make revenue more seamlessly.

Researching this book has been fun to do. I hope you will find it entertaining and easy to understand while reading.

# Chapter 1: Understanding YouTube

## What Is YouTube?

YouTube is a platform that came into fruition in 2005. It is one of the most recognized video websites you can find on the internet today. Individuals share and upload numerous videos on this platform regularly. Some of these include How to guides to amateur videos of dogs among many others.

As long as you have an internet connection, you will be able to distribute content on YouTube. This is the case irrespective of if you own a company with a massive budget or you are just an individual who owns a video camera.

Google owns YouTube, and the platform is one of its most recognized peripheral properties. Initially, YouTube was the pioneer video sharing website on the internet for large scale videos. What's more, it is available in almost all nations and comes in more than 40 diverse languages. Any individual can upload content on YouTube, which results in a fantastic array of videos.

What are the Major Functions of YouTube?

- Provides users with the ability to search for videos and watch them

- Allows you to create your own YouTube channel

- Let's users upload videos to their channel

- Let's users comment, like and share other videos

- It will enable users to follow and subscribe to other YouTube users and channels

- Let's users create playlists to group and organize videos

## How Do You Watch Videos on YouTube?

To get results tailored to you, all you have to do is

comment on other videos or create playlists. Users need to create a YouTube account or link a global Google account you own with the new YouTube account.

This enables YouTube to learn what you prefer. For example, assuming you search for videos that aid you in training your dog. The next time you open the YouTube page, if your Google account is signed in, YouTube will automatically display additional videos that teach you how to train your dog.

This feature aids YouTube in personalizing what they display to users, so they provide a more significant user experience. But, if you would prefer YouTube doesn't save your choices, all you need to do is to sign out of your Google account before utilizing YouTube.

There are numerous ways of finding what you want to view on YouTube. They include:

- Browse using keyword phrase or keyword

- Find videos in categories and topics

- Filter videos in categories and topics

- Check out the charts ranking for trending videos in any category

If you see a video, you are interested in; you will also find a comment section underneath the video. Here you will be able to say what you feel. Lots of videos come with comment sections where users can say what they feel. They will also be able to like or dislike a video. Some video owners disable this section. This is solely based on the choice of the specific YouTube user.

## How Do You Share Videos You Love?

If you come across a video you fancy and want to share it with your friends and loved ones, there are a host of options for sharing. YouTube offers Email alongside other major services for social networking. What's more, you will have the capacity to share the URL of the video or attach the video.

Just click the share button underneath a video, and you will be offered numerous options to share it with family and friends.

Lots of YouTube videos end up going viral with this method. Viral videos are those that are viewed and shared by a considerable number of people. Lots of viral videos have view counts in millions and sometimes billions.

## Storing Videos to Use Later

YouTube is rich with content. As a result, the service offers you a range of options to save videos you like. You can create video playlists with ease and stream without interruption.

To add a video to your list, all you need to do is select the 'add to' button and pick the list you want the video attached to. You will also have the option of creating another list.

Another method of keeping up with individuals who post videos you like is to subscribe to the account of the user. This ensures each time they upload anything, and you get a notification. It is an easy method of keeping videos you like bookmarked so you can watch them whenever you want.

## How Do You Upload Your Videos to YouTube?

YouTube has ensured it is easy to upload videos. All you have to do is locate the video on your computer, input the critical fields like keywords, topic, and description before clicking upload.

You will get a notification via email the instant the video has been uploaded completely. Dependent on your internet connection speed and the video size, it may require some seconds to a few minutes to upload videos.

### *Finding What You Like On YouTube*

Irrespective of what you might be in search of, ranging from reviews, funny videos among others, it is available on YouTube. It is an excellent location to explore your existing interests and finding more that you can begin to cultivate.

## Benefits of Using YouTube

There is a range of benefits that come from using YouTube. We will be taking a look at a few of these below;

### *Take Advantage of The Enormous Traffic on YouTube*

Online video is growing significantly, with more than 3 billion videos viewed each day. If you utilize YouTube for business, you will be able to reach your audience with ease, both by developing videos and running adverts on the videos of other individuals.

Other reasons YouTube traffic can benefit you include:

- YouTube is the 2nd biggest search engine. It is also the 3rd most visited site around the globe following Facebook and

YouTube

- Every month, 1 billion individuals pay a visit to YouTube around the world

- Every 60 seconds, there are over 90 hours of videos uploaded on YouTube

- Platforms for video-streaming like YouTube have become so large that you are sure to locate a category of individuals who will become your customers and fans. This is possible so far you teach, entertain and offer solutions to their issues.

## *Using YouTube For Marketing Will Aid You in Getting Found on Google*

With the help of Google universal search, news, videos, books, images alongside local searches are merged in Google search results. This is to offer the most significant information for individuals searching.

You may observe that videos are popping up

more frequently in the search results of Google. This portrays that Google sees videos to be as crucial as text-only pages.

You can exploit this by writing articles of high-quality on your website and developing videos that complement it on YouTube. In doing this, backlinks would be built to your site, which means you will show up on Google more frequently when people search.

By using YouTube as an aspect of your business marketing strategy, you are also enhancing your website's authority. The more authoritative your site is in the eyes of Google, the higher your page ranking will be in the search results.

By utilizing YouTube as part of your marketing strategy for your business, you're also increasing your website authority. The more authoritative your website is in Google's eyes, the higher the ranking all your pages will be in the search results.

## *Your Content Lives On Forever*

Utilizing YouTube for your business can aid you in re-purposing content you have created already without having to invest in costly equipment or spend too much time.

Re-purposing content you created already is an efficient means of content marketing. This is because you will be able to get across to an audience that will fancy that specific kind of content.

For example, you can re-purpose a blog post on your website into various formats which include:

- Presentations

- Podcasts

- Video Series

- Infographics

With this approach, you will be able to develop no less than four pieces of content from only one idea. It would also result in an audience which is engaged and can take in the information you offer to them with ease.

## *Nurture Your Audience Around the Globe*

This is one of the most significant benefits of utilizing YouTube for your business. Creating video continuously gives you access to new visitors who may never have crossed paths your business through any other means.

Using YouTube, you will be able to reach a global viewer base even if you do not know how to speak more than one language. If your native language is English, you have the upper hand because if you are unable to produce or write excellent content, it would be hard to capture the English speaking market which makes 30 percent of all the views on YouTube.

Additionally, if you can add closed captions to your videos, you will also be able to get across to new audiences because you are providing for individuals with diverse requirements.

Research now proves that videos having closed-captions get 4 percent more subscribers and views that those that do not have them.

Also, it is essential to add numerous CTAs in your videos, alongside annotations linking to:

- Content on your site

- Other videos

- Services and products on offer

### *Develop Your Email List Using YouTube*

This is another benefit of utilizing YouTube for business. You will be able to grow your email list as you keep offering engaging and valuable content.

Utilize software that can aid you in integrating a sign-up from straight into your YouTube videos. A video can be temporarily stopped for a viewer to input his/her email address information and subscribe to your email list, before going on.

With this approach, it is seamless to develop your email list, while offering engaging content your audience will enjoy.

### *Your Viewers Will Help in Promoting You and Purchase from You*

Videos that have a personal feel will aid in enhancing conversions. Individuals purchase from those they feel they can rely on, and this trust is developed when you relate to them emotionally.

Research proves that for generic companies and professional services if you are pushing viewers to a landing page using a video of an individual in the organization talking about the service or product, it can drastically enhance your list of sales and leads.

### *It lets your Earn Revenue Using AdSense for Video*

Regularly creating video content offers you the chance of earning some cash straight from your videos using Google AdSense video program.

If you are not aware, the following are a few facts regarding this:

- More than 2 million creators of content from over 20 countries around the world are earning revenue just from YouTube Videos

- Numerous channels make six figures yearly

- You can utilize Google AdSense and AdWords for video simultaneously to earn some cash from your video campaigns as well

- Creating video content frequently offers you the chance to earn some revenue straight from your videos. You can do this using the video program offered by Google AdSense. This implies that you will be able to run AdWords promotions for your videos while earning cash by letting others place adverts on your videos,

As you can observe, YouTube is an excellent platform for devolving your business and audience in a range of ways.

### *Develop Your Audience Internationally*

This is another significant benefit of utilizing YouTube for business. Developing content in the form of videos on a platform designed for videos can open the path to new clients who may never have come across your services or business normally. Using YouTube, you will be able to reach a global audience even if you don't speak more than one language if you can authorize YouTube to support subtitles in diverse languages.

Also, to broaden the range of individuals you can reach, you will also be able to add a closed caption which allows you to cater to individuals with various requirements.

### *You Will Have More Visibility on Google*

A search engine like Google, asides from picking up your articles also pick images, videos and a host of others. The more content you produce and the more they vary, you will be able to enhance the possibility of you being found by search engines.

One thing you have to note is making sure you utilize descriptions and title names which are significant. This is because those are the things search engines tend to use in making your video show up as a relevant link when a person is searching for information along similar lines. You can equally add short blog posts that complement the video, and propose that readers watch your video for additional information which then directs them to your account on

YouTube.

By integrating YouTube as an aspect of your business marketing strategy, you will also be enhancing your website authority. The ranking of your pages in search results is dependent on how authoritative Google feels your website is. Ensure you keep this in mind when developing your objectives.

Below are a few tips for utilizing YouTube to enhance your website Authority:

- Provide your audience with more choices to consume

- Share your videos on various social media outlets

- Link your domain name with your YouTube channel

- Get owners of other websites to embed your videos on their sites

## Ways to Make Money from YouTube

Similar to being a blogger or influencer on Instagram, your audience may give you the capacity to earn more. However, it is the creation of numerous streams of revenue that aids you in actually making cash.

The great news is that there are a lot of methods of earning cash on YouTube which include:

### *Create Online Courses*

Online courses are one of the best ways for you to diversify your earnings on your YouTube channel. Why? The online market is growing significantly, as a matter of fact, by 2025, it meant to get as high as $325 billion.

Lots of marketers are beginning to take advantage of the online courses platform as a means of monetizing content. Now, more than ever before, people desire to learn and online courses are ideal digital products for addressing this need.

The great part is, you don't require lots of

expertise or experience to begin. With the help of online courses, you can exploit your specialty and knowledge to sell courses to an interested audience and draw in new traffic.

It is one of the top methods of creating your constant stream of income which is dependent on you as opposed to a sponsor. It's a better option because a sponsor can back out at any time and demonetize you instantly.

Online courses are crucial for YouTubers for a variety of reasons:

- YouTubers are excellent in developing video content

- They already have engaged fans

- YouTubers have an in-built marketing platform

Even better, online courses are products that you produce once and can sell multiple times. Just by placing a link in each of your video description or a quick mention in every second video can assist you in maintaining a continuous stream of revenue.

## How Can You Promote Your Course on YouTube?

The subsequent problems lot of YouTubers face after creating online courses is how to promote them on their channel.

Lots of viewers won't watch a commercial lasting for 5 minutes for your online course. However, they will view a video which offers value while preparing your audience to purchase your online course.

For example, if you created a course on How to train your dog, you may create a video called 'Basic skills every dog trainer needs to know.' And you will go over the dog training basics.

At the completion of the video, indicate that you have to complete an online course that covers all the necessary skills that develop the foundation of becoming a reliable dog trainer. You can also add that you are offering a discount for viewers who purchase it via the video. Offer your viewers a coupon code and inform them that they will also be getting a bonus straight from you when they use the code. This bonus can be a little extra like an eBook they can download, or a one-on-one 10 minutes consultation with you for the initial customers via a Skype call.

The idea is to ensure that you are not only selling. Instead, you have to;

- Offer value

- Ensure your views feel you are providing them with a unique offer

- Thank your viewers for watching and offering their support

- Spinning your course is a means for you to:

- Connect with your fans better

- Support your YouTube channel so you will be able to develop extra content that will aid your audience in getting more eager about your course and enhancing the possibility of them offering you support.

## Why Is It Essential You Create An Online Course?

Lots of individuals choose to create online courses because they are aware of how lucrative they are. Although the idea of making revenue is appealing, that is one of the numerous reasons why you need to develop an online course.

Other reasons include:

- **They offer full-time or part-time income.** It is easier to monetize a course on your YouTube channel. This is because every individual has something he/she wants to learn.

- **Every individual has some**

**knowledge to impact.** We all have online courses in us. This is because we have our unique passion, hobbies, and skills we can transform into online courses. You don't have to be that experienced to create a profitable online course.

- **They are assets you can reuse.** The instant you develop your online course for your audience, you will be able to reformat, repurpose and resell the course as many times as you want. You will be able to earn from an online course today and continue making a profit from it for years in the future.

- **You are already an expert.** Lots of individuals are worried that they don't have the proper qualification to teach because they are not experts in the field. But it has been proven that even the most experienced teachers are just a few steps ahead of those they teach.

If you were a newbie six months back, you are usually much better suited for teaching a topic than individuals who became experts years back.

- **You will be able to assist vast amounts of individuals' simultaneously.** Online courses provide content in a format which lots of people can easily understand. It is also straightforward. What is more, you will be able to reach a considerable number of individuals and offer lots of transformations.

- **They offer high ROI.** If you have already created content and have an online audience, online courses are the fastest means of making revenue off the work you have done already. Even if you are just starting, the time you would have to invest in online courses is not as much as what you would in a video or blog series.

- **You can charge extra.** Education is valuable to a lot of people. For this reason, people will always be willing to pay more. You can increase the amount you charge if you are confident of the value you are offering.

## Become A YouTube Partner & Earn Cash from Ads

Ads are probably the first stream of revenue you would try out. First, you will have to become a YouTube partner. You can do this easily in the Creator Studio area of your YouTube account by heading to the Channel menu to authenticate your account and get monetization enabled.

After becoming a partner, you will require an AdSense account to become a part of Google's advertising network to get paid and view ad revenue reports.

The instant you are through, you will observe a green dollar sign close to your videos when you open the video manager. This shows that it has been activated for monetization.

It is not difficult to set up. However, advertising as a partner on YouTube is not the most profitable revenue stream you can establish for yourself.

## Why Do You Need To Look Past Ads For Income?

Recently, YouTube got a lot of criticism due to its choice to be more transparent as regards advertising and what kind of content is classified as advertiser-friendly.

Lots of creators believed they would lose out of the revenue gotten from ads which aided in supporting their channel as a result of their kind of content.

As stated by YouTube, your content could get taken off Ads if it consists of

- Material which is sexually suggestive, including sexual humor or partial nakedness

- Unsuitable language which includes: Vulgar language, profanity, and harassment

- Promotion of substances related to drug including the use and sales of such items

- Sensitive or controversial events and topics which include subjects that have to do with tragedies, war, and political conflicts even if no graphic image is displayed

But the fact is; YouTube has been demonetizing content it does not feel is advertiser-friendly since 2012 using an automated process. YouTubers were already losing ad revenues because sometimes their videos would get demonetized without notification and without their knowledge. However, it is better now, as creators get a notification when this occurs and can contest videos that were excluded by mistake from the advertising network of YouTube.

Advertisements may be a common method for creators to generate passive income, but the clause is that YouTube is allowed to keep a 45 percent share of revenue made from ads. In summary, if you want to be a YouTuber, you need to check out other streams of revenue to keep this hobby going.

So let us take a look at other options.

### *Earn Cash on YouTube Through the Sales of Products*

The sales of products like tote bags, coffee mugs among a host of others offer more benefits asides revenue. It enhances your exposure by placing your online personality and brand into the offline world. It also makes the relationship between your fans and yourself much more in-depth as they buy into what you do.

The sales of branded clothes are easier than it might look initially. You will be able to order budget-friendly designs tailored for specific items like t-shirt using freelance websites like Freelancer or Upwork.

And when it has to do with handling customers and orders, you will be able to integrate your stores on the providers of print-on-demand services that take care of all the customer support, fulfillment and shipping. This lets you enjoy all the advantages of a drop shipping business which requires little effort from you.

As an alternative, you can collaborate with an existing merchandising network for creators like DFTBA. But, you will have to compete with other YouTubers in the market. You will also have limited control when it comes to providing discounts, adding products, embedding your content, and all the perks that come alongside being the owner of your website.

You can also go further by selling and

manufacturing your own distinct products and power it with your YouTube channel. There are game companies that sell their games using How-to or game review videos.

As a user of YouTube who has already attained a following, you would have two benefits from the beginning that other store owners would envy;

- A content platform that drives traffic continuously to your store

- The trust of your audience which you have earned already by serving them your own kind of content free of charge.

### *Crowdfund Your Subsequent Creative Project*

When funding is all that is limiting your idea from execution, a great way of making this happen is through crowdfunding.

Irrespective of if you require assistance purchasing better equipment or covering other costs of production, you can reach out to your audience and the crowdfunding community to help out if you have a fascinating and compelling idea.

Lots of creative projects which were crowdfunded tend to provide a sneak view that gets individuals intrigued. So you need to consider making a video which explains your project or provides a taste of how it would seem like.

Well-known crowdfunding websites which have a great track record of campaigns from YouTubers consist of Indiegogo and Kickstarter.

Get Support for your work from your YouTube Audience using streams of Fan Funding to get donations from your audience. As a YouTube creator, you are offering your voice to the web without compelling your audience to pay a fee. So, if your content is excellent, your audience may be obligated to support you frequently.

Lots of platforms for fan funding provide creators with another location for individuals to find their content and a method of engaging their most loyal fans and offer them a prize for their support.

Some popular options for fan funding include:

- YouTube's Fan Funding: Here, you will typically be able to create a place where viewers would be able to donate whatever amount they desire to contribute at any time. However, to do this, your account needs to be set-up for advertising.

- Tipeee: allows you to attain a mix of continuous and one time donations.

### *Offer the Media A License to Your Content*

If you create a video which goes viral and has an enormous appeal like say a funny clip which features your cat, you will be able to license your content in exchange for cash.

Morning shows, TV news outlets, online news websites and other kinds of creators may contact you regarding the rights to utilize your videos if they go viral.

Alternatively, you will be able to list your videos in marketplaces like Junken Media where it would be less complicated for the appropriate individuals to locate and buy your content.

## *Work Alongside Brands as An Affiliate or Influencer*

In the coming years, Influencer marketing is going to be one of the most crucial means of advertisement.

Brands are beginning to invest lots of cash in influencer marketing, spending a considerable chunk of their usually massive advertisement budgets on influencers who have their audience loyalty already.

This creates a tremendous opportunity to tap from if you are a creator and can negotiate the appropriate deals. According to YouTube influencer and marketing expert, it is recommended you establish your flat fee by checking out the number of average views you get on your video and multiplying it by 4-16 percent for each view which is similar to what lots of companies would choose to pay for ads on YouTube.

Depending on your content quality, your audience demographics, and how profitable and unique your niche is, you may have the capacity to negotiate a great deal.

The critical thing to know about content sponsored by a brand is to be completely transparent. You should not endorse a product you don't believe in or like, and you should also be straightforward to your audience as regards why you are doing it.

There are a host of influencer marketplaces you will be able to add your channel to so you will be discovered by both small and large brands which include:

- Famebit: Offers a broad range of brands

you can work alongside. You require 5,000 followers to be a part of this platform.

- Grapevine Logic: This is one of the most recognized marketplaces for influencers. You need just 1000 followers to become a part of this platform

- Channel Pages: Let's you form collaborations with YouTubers alongside other brands.

There are influencer marketplaces which provide you with free products, while others are known to have large brands who are eager to pay you more. Exploit the opportunities you find suitable, but ensure you list yourself in numerous locations so you can ensure your channel has peak visibility.

As an alternative, you can become a brand affiliate and make passive income via commissions from each sale that comes in from your channel. This is a great option especially if you are a product reviewer on your YouTube channel. Since this method does not pose any risk to the brand, there are usually not many requirements for starting this.

Well, known affiliate programs consist of Click Bank which offers 1percent to as much as 70 percent on more depending on what is set by the vendor. Amazon's Affiliate network is another great option which gives you the opportunity to make as much as 10 percent for each sale.

You can also contact brands in the same niche as you currently running affiliate programs, which is quite common in the e-commerce environment.

### *Ways to Sell Without Being A Nuisance to Your Audience*

Lots of the strategies above for monetizing have to do with the promotion of products or campaigns. You still have to ensure your audience knows about all of this without damaging your content's integrity.

For a lot of creators, selling out to their audience

is a real issue. However, if you need something, you need to ask.

There are a host of placements you can select from to promote your campaigns or product which are:

- **Place a CTA or Videos**

CTA or call to action is very simple but crucial. It goes something like:

*"If you enjoyed this video, then subscribe and hit the like button."*

Lots of YouTubers add a call to action similar to this beneath their videos to improve their viewership. If you suggest the proposed action you want your audience to take, there is a higher likelihood of them taking it.

You can utilize this method to direct the attention of your audience to an opportunity for generating revenue.

- **Place Timely YouTube Cards In Your**

### Videos

Irrespective of if you are promoting your products or it is the deal you had with a brand, YouTube cards provide an appealing method of getting the attention of viewers.

You will be able to set them to show up at the best moment of the vide when they are most significant and not as distracting to enhance their effects.

- **Place Links In Your Video Descriptions**

You divert views to your store, campaign or other aspects of your online presence focused on revenue by placing links in your video descriptions.

- **Use Other Platforms In Promoting Your Offer**

Because YouTube is hosting your content does not imply you should not exploit the other channels for distribution available to you.

- Promote new discounts or campaigns via Facebook, Instagram, Twitter or any of your other profiles. The more locations you place your messages, the higher the possibility of it been seen. So, it is always an excellent choice to grow your following on social media past YouTube.

## Ways Your Business Can Use YouTube To Reach Your Audience

Reaching your audience is crucial on YouTube. There are lots of ways you can do this which include:

### *Show the Testimonials of Customers*

If your business has been running for a long time and you have attained the respect of lots of loyal clients or customers, using a YouTube video to display some of these organizations or people offering real testimonials for your services or products can be a very efficient and low-cost sales and promotional tool.

## *Use A Call to Action*

YouTube lets you speak with your audience directly. For this reason, you will be able to utilize your videos to urge users to take a particular action after viewing your video.

A CTA is a request for individuals to take an instant action like visiting your site, subscribe to your channel, like the video, share your video link with their contacts, make a purchase or a donation among others.

For organizations selling merchandise, a great call to action is to add a link in your video which redirects to a website offering a special offer or money-saving coupon for what you are trying to sell. This could be a percentage off the buying price for a limited period, and a buy one get one free offer or free shipping.

Clarify it in the video that the offer is exclusive to individuals viewing the footage and ensure the special offer is available the instant the video ends.

## *Develop Mindless Entertainment, But Utilize Product Placement*

Lots of individuals head to YouTube to get entertained because the platform contains lots of shocking and funny videos. You and your organization can become a part of this trend and create videos that provide mindless entertainment while simultaneously adding subtle marketing messages or product placements as regards your product or organization in the videos.

For this form of video, it is essential that you are creative, as your post has to be funny, unique, engaging and entertaining. Remember that the key is using a soft-sell approach.

### *Share or Promote an Event Highlight*

Normally, any event that you or your company partakes in takes place in the real world in some part of the world and will pull in crowds from the surrounding environment.

But, when you share videos taken at events that recently took place, you will have the chance of sharing it with the world. Displaying shortened footage from a prior event can aid in generating interest in future events and increase attendance.

## *Stream A Live Event Using YouTube*

Asides from filming an event, shortening and editing videos and publishing it on your YouTube channel, you can broadcast it live using YouTube live. By transmitting life, your audience can stream your video in real time.

In essence, as the event takes place, your audience can see it live. This means there is no margin for mistakes. Businesses can utilize live streaming in broadcasting a press conference, product launch or unique event.

## *Pay Popular YouTubers To Feature Your Products in Their Videos*

As opposed to producing a video yourself, promoting it and utilizing all of the financial resources needed to build an audience and promote your videos, you can pay a YouTuber with a considerable following to place product placements for your services or product into their videos.

The subscribers of these popular YouTubers are usually quite loyal. For this reason, when they endorse a product, their subscribers typically want to try out such players. Majority of the YouTubers appeal to a precise demographic.

So, if you are about launching a gaming chair, for example, look for a YouTuber who is a gaming guru with a large following. Paying for product placement is an easy and fast way of promoting your product and having it seen by lots of targeted viewers.

# Chapter 2. Determining Who You Are On YouTube

## How Do You Develop A Personal Brand?

Personal branding is huge nowadays. This is the era of the individual and similar to other things surrounding them, the individual is subjected to branding. In this increasingly competitive world, it is essential that you be your brand.

Let's assume you are in search of a Job. You are already aware that most hiring managers would do a quick search of your name on google before calling on you for an interview. What are the things they will find? If you create a personal brand, they will see high-quality content underneath your name. However, if you don't have a personal brand, only those silly images you have been posting over the years on Facebook will show up.

YouTube is an excellent platform for developing

your brand. We will be looking at some tips that can help you begin.

## *Understand the Brand and Yourself*

The most difficult question for most people is: Who are you? This is what you have to answer via your YouTube channel. Locate the individuals you desire everyone to see. Ensure your activity relates to your personal and professional objectives. Say, for example, you are a makeup artist trying to pull people to your class or website, you share makeup tips and the best kinds of makeup accessories among others. Same goes if you are a sales expert, you will share tips and experiences for the community.

YouTube gives you the chance to upload videos on any subject. You can utilize that chance to portray yourself as a professional in your field.

But there is something crucial you should note; This is not precisely a channel for promoting your business. You are promoting yourself. What this means is that your personality has to show and you have to ensure everyone knows who you are.

### *Create the Profile*

What name are you going to pick for your channel? Going with your name is not a bad idea. However, you can also create a fantastic channel name that would hold its own.

Below are some other things to note when creating the channel:

- Offer your bio in the About section explaining what the channel entails. Add links to your Facebook, Twitter, Instagram pages and LinkedIn profile. You can also include a link to your official website if you own one. Yes, it's essential that you have a personal site if you are trying to develop a brand centered on your name.

- Tweak the settings. YouTube lets you set the most recent video as the one that will feature on your channel. Creating tags and titles for the channel is also possible. Also, you can customize the structure in a way that benefits you.

## *Keep A Logical Progression*

You won't be uploading random videos relating to topics that pop-up in your head. Personal branding is a process which is continuous.

Lots of coaches use YouTube to publish brief training videos as a part of their training programs. Email messages containing private links to videos will be sent to subscribers. It is a technique lots of coaches use. They promote videos after creating programs in a logical progression. You will be able to locate playlists and can also use long hours viewing them.

This is an example to learn from. When you are developing a personal brand, consider logical progression and consistency always. Develop playlists and call on your audience to check out other relevant videos after they view one of them.

The more they see of you, the more powerful an impression your audience will have of your brand.

### *The Branding Is Important*

According to Roberta Collings, a writer, filming videos is not adequate. There should be something people recognize you for. Having an intro is essential.

If you check out some of the popular channels on YouTube, you will observe they begin with an intro. Ensure you do something similar for your videos. In essence, you need to hire the services of an expert to edit the material in a manner that is professional if you don't know how to go about it.

You want a snappy, brief intro as well as videos that are on point. Asides from the intro, you require other details that will aid you in building a personal using YouTube videos. Your style is crucial — how you speak and the strange topics you cover. The humor you utilize. All these are an aspect of your brand. Consider an unusual plot that makes you stand out from the others.

### *Ensure You Are Consistent*

Nobody will subscribe to your channel because you uploaded one great video. They want to view more content, so they will be aware you have amazing things to provide. When this happens, YouTube will continue recommending your most recent videos to subscribers. This way, you will have a continuous flow of audience depending on you.

Create a publishing schedule for your videos and stick to it. The more content you offer, the more powerful your brand would get.

Filming videos can be a scary experience. It is like exposing your weakest areas to a massive audience. However, it is a fantastic experience that places you in front of a continuous flow of feedback. You can learn from this and keep growing.

### *Be True To Your Niche*

You'll most likely locate lots of channels on YouTube that share various kinds of videos. For example, a channel may consist of cat videos, reviews, music mixes and talks on a range of topics.

When you post random videos, it is not an example of good personal branding. You need to be focused.

According to a Marketing professional from BestEssay, Johnny Paules: You have to ensure your viewers continue heading back to your channel by keeping a logical flow between your videos.

It is almost impossible getting returning viewers and subscribers from one viral video. When you are making efforts to develop a personal brand, you need to be consistent. You want people to know you and also follow your advice. This is possible if you stick to your chosen niche and share videos that are valuable to your viewers.

## Locating Your Niche on YouTube

With more than 200 hours of videos uploaded on YouTube each minute, making an excellent video is no longer enough. If you desire to be found and want to have the capacity to monetize your YouTube channel, it is vital for you to find your niche.

If you mean business and want to transform your YouTube Channel into a lucrative market, you need a niche. The niche should not only allow you to do things you have a passion for, but it should also get you the views you require. The ideal niche is one that your audience is searching for already. Something not too competitive and still lets you showcase your knowledge and passion.

Finding a niche that is perfect for you on YouTube is not easy. You will require a bit of self-awareness, creativity and a great deal of thought.

So you have to be ready to invest some energy and time into the process.

If you initially fail to get it right, take a few steps back and determine where you took a wrong turn and try again. Now, let us take a look at how you can begin searching for your perfect niche on YouTube.

## How to Find Your Niche?

If you want to begin searching for your niche, there are some ways of doing this. You could begin by putting down your hobbies and searching for trends with those. You can also think about the kinds of videos you love making most.

How would your knowledge of a specific topic or what you do for a living help in inspiring your channel? The key is to find out where you can provide something interesting or unique to YouTube. Hopefully, by merging your knowledge, hobbies, and passion into one massive ball of intelligence.

For example, if you are interested in cooking tutorials but spend a year moving around Mexico, why not do Mexican inspired cooking? Or if you are passionate about footwear but work as a business consultant, why not provide content about great shoe to wear for business meetings?

The amazing spot where video genre meets with your talents and passion is where your niche lies.

## Why Is Finding Your Niche Crucial?

Locating a niche is all about providing your viewers with what they wish to see. Imagine you are a plastic surgeon and all your videos are about plastic surgery. Then one day, you travel to London and randomly post a video about traveling around London. Your video was viral, you got over 50k views, but you were able to get just about ten subscribers to your channel. Why?

The answer to this is not complicated. If the people who checked out your video on traveling in London, and thought about subscribing, they would have checked out your channel and saw none of your prior videos related to this topic. Irrespective of the fact that you uploaded a great video, you did not seem relevant to them, so they chose not to bother.

From the subscriber's point of view, they want to know what you are about. They want to feel sure that if they subscribe to your channel, they will be attaining a lot of amazing and quality things that have to do with what they have an interest in. Having a focused and clear niche will give you the chance to do this for them.

## How to Narrow Down Your YouTube Niche

The more precise and smaller your focus, the less difficult it would be for you to attain and keep subscribers. If you are into phone reviews, why not make it even more focused by doing it about Samsung phone reviews? If your niche is about game reviews, why not make it more focused by doing a PS4 game review channel.

When you narrow down your area of focus, it will

be less complicated to market and appeal to your audience. When an individual from your target audience locates your channel, they are going to be like; great, this is precisely what I was looking for, and they will view, share, interact and like your videos with more enthusiasm than someone who is not that interested.

## How Do You Locate Your Niche?

If you still do not know how to pinpoint the perfect niche for your channel on YouTube, this is what we will be covering here.

Below are some crucial things to consider when searching for your niche which will aid you in getting where you desire to be;

### *What Do You Have A Passion For? What Are You Great At?*

Create a list of stuff you are great at. This is one of those times you can be proud of it. Consider the stuff others always request your assistance for and those things you are confident of.

Understanding the areas you are talented in is an excellent area to begin.

PONY Syndrome is an excellent example of this. She is a makeup artist popular for her transformation of Tailor Swift. She noticed that lots of individuals always came to her for advice on makeup, so she began to make videos on her methods. Skip forward a few years, and she has more than e million subscribers and a very lucrative channel on YouTube.

You may not see yourself as an expert in a particular field, but it is often the exciting mix of things you are passionate about and your talents that make you stand out.

Subscribers who find your videos useful have a higher likelihood of coming back to you numerous times. Most individuals enjoy having a great laugh after going through entertaining videos. But the channels that are more likely to make the most cash are those people find extremely helpful.

## *Does Your Potential Niche Have An Audience?*

The instant you know your potential niche. You have to ensure there are individuals out there who would watch it. To try this out, imagine a video you could create on your niche and try searching for it on YouTube. If the results are a lot, your niche is possibly not adequately focused.

You should be searching for something in the middle of both extremes. If you observe that a few popular channels have made one or two videos relating to your topic, but did not place a focus on it, you can be confident that an audience is out there but with a reasonable competition. You can also search for something that has a lot of websites or blog posts about and be the first person to move the content to YouTube.

For example, if you were to search; Phone unboxing. You will find a lot of results. Many of these would be from influencers who have already established themselves and taken over the market. So for a newcomer, remaining in business may be difficult.

This does not imply you should abandon the idea entirely, but it means you will need to work twice as much to make your channel unique. With some originality, you will eventually get there.

### *What Will You Do That Would Be Different From Other Channels?*

There is a lot of content out there to check out. If you are not exciting, you would most likely not make your millions. Viewers are aware that there is quality, fun content out there, and they will look for someone more entertaining and skillful than you are if you are too bland for their liking. People look for information on YouTube, but personality makes them stick around. So ensure you place some of yours into all you do.

There are numerous ways of bringing engagement and excitement to your YouTube channel. Consider the following;

- The way you speak

- How you look

- How you make your introduction

- Your overall concept

- The affects you utilize in your videos

Once you can consider all this, you will have an infinite possibility of developing exciting and distinct videos. But if standing out from the crowd is your goal, you will need to be creative.

## *Would You Be Able To Make Revenue In This Niche?*

Lots of people begin a YouTube channel with the aim of earning millions from what they do. But, if you start with the wrong niche, you could go under before you even begin.

Researching if it is possible to monetize the niche you choose is important. Below are ways to find out:

- Will an organization likely offer you sponsorship to utilize its products?

- Will you be able to create a side hustle along with your channel?

Sponsorships are very lucrative, but they are not easy to attain. Is there an organization with products you could utilize in your videos? If there are, is there a YouTuber they prefer and are already sponsoring? For a side business, you can look for anything from selling products through Amazon through an affiliate deal to providing one-to-one consultancy. The crucial thing is that you should have a plan from the beginning.

How many topics can you come up with to make videos on for your channel? If you can't come up with at least ten topics from your head, that is not a great sign. You are going to require lots of inspiration and ideas for your YouTube videos. If you are already battling to come up with things you can do, imagine how much the struggle will be a few years down the line.

Your niche has to inspire you completely. You also need to love it. This is because there is a huge possibility that you will be stuck with this niche. You will be making lots of videos that relate to this topic for years to come.

Are you confident that this topic would intrigue you the coming year? Will the passion you have for the content survive the test of time? Try to determine the changes that will occur in your life over the coming years and if you will find your niche suitable going forward.

## Popular YouTube Niches

There are a few niches on YouTube which won't give you as many issues monetizing in comparison to others. This does not imply that you should limit yourself to these niches alone, but if you do not have any inspiration, these areas of focus are great places to begin your search.

## Funny Animals

Preventing yourself from seeing funny animals on the web is not possible. People love to look at cute animals especially when they are doing something unusual.

YouTube also has a significant number of channels focusing on funny animals. Some show videos of actual animals clinching the limelight. Others come in the form of animation like Simons Cat.

Of course, there are also a host of serious animal channels. National Geographic videos is an example of this and features the popular David Attenborough.

## Video Game Walkthroughs

PewDiePie is the top influencer who rules this category. Young males who are the most popular kinds of gamers were the first kind of people to fall for YouTube. So it should not be surprising that there is a range of channels dedicated to video gaming.

A walkthrough is a typical kind of gaming video. Here, an individual plays a game and leaves comments as he progresses through the game. One of the major reasons Minecraft is popular even though it has ancient graphics is that the game can be modded with ease and filmmakers utilize this functionality in their videos, playing as modded characters.

There can be massive engagement between makers of videos alongside their supporters. There is also a possibility of live play sessions.

## How to Tutorials and Guides

There are three kinds of learning styles which are:

- Auditory – by hearing

- Visual – by seeing

- Kinesthetic – By doing

All individuals learn using a mixture of these

methods, but lots of individuals find that one of the methods is less complicated than others. Great teachers try to utilize a combination of all methods while teaching.

Why it will be difficult teaching in a video kinetically, it is an excellent medium for individuals who enjoy both auditory and visual learning experiences. A video which is well structured and inspires you to work hand in hand with your presentation, can be significant to those who prefer Kinesthetic method of learning.

There are a range of how to videos on YouTube. You are most likely going to locate something to aid you in doing almost anything that comes to mind. The benefit of these kinds of videos is that they could last a long time. A video would only get out of date when the activity changes or gets outdated.

If you feel there is something you know and you can teach it to other people in a manner they would find entertaining while still learning, this is an excellent niche for you.

## *Reviews of Products*

Nowadays, individuals head to the internet when they want to make a purchase. They want to find out what other individuals feel about the product they want to buy.

YouTube is similar to other social media platforms in this aspect. Individuals troop to their trusted channels to see how they feel about the range of products they review.

According to polls, consumers have a higher likelihood of buying something if they find positive reviews online. It is mostly dependent on the product, but YouTube is the ideal medium for lots of products. People find a review more relatable if they can see the product being utilized with their own eyes. This can be said about test driving a car, applying make-up or using a new electronic appliance.

## *Vlogs*

A blog is short for weblog, but most individuals don't remember that anymore. A web-based log was a kind of internet diary where a person spoke about his/her daily activities. Blogs have since diversified, but you can still locate some individuals writing happily about their daily activities and the things they did the day before.

Vlogs are video bogs, and it has the same concept to what the blog used to be. They are a diary in video form.

But because you are doing this on YouTube, they are not as hidden as a diary in your room, so it has more engaging content. Vlogs, similar to a journal, utilize unscripted dialog and usually seems like a genuine look into the mind of the video maker. Often, the focus of vlogs is on one topic.

Vlogs are usually the same as a YouTube reality show. Individuals get the opportunity to see the vlogger's life. Similar to a reality show on television, it can amass some high number of views. Some vlogs channels have a reasonably high following.

If you feel you live an exciting life and would be able to share it with the world, while keeping them engaged, vlogging is the way to go.

### Comedy Videos

Some individuals create sketch videos and comedy to keep their viewers entertained. A sense of humor differs between individuals, but there are lots of comedy videos on the web that you are sure to find one that fits your style.

Comedy videos are some of the most distributed, and some of these often find their way to other social media outlets. This is one that has the most possibility to go viral.

There are YouTube comedy channels that amass more viewing than lots of comedy shows on Television. If you think you can make funny videos certain to keep people entertained, this is the way to go.

## *Hauls/Shopping Sprees*

Lots of women particularly, love to watch others go on shopping sphere for items they themselves can only purchase in their wildest dreams. You may be unable to go high-end bag shopping on your own and purchase a few pairs of brand-name bags, but you may enjoy viewing another person do it.

Shopping spree videos, traditionally called haul videos, emphasize on individuals shopping for specific items. These kinds of videos are commonly in the fashion, lifestyle and beauty channels.

These videos offer a clear chance for brands that want to partake in influencer marketing. So far, the products being bought fit the kinds of products that viewer of the channel desire.

## *Unboxing Videos*

Surprisingly, a considerable amount of individuals love watching another person take out a new product from a box.

This is a kind of extension of product review and shopping spree videos. They sort of fit during the purchase process and the act of utilizing and reviewing the product.

The love we have for these kinds of videos is similar to the love a child has for Christmas morning. Half the entertainment comes from unwrapping the gifts and having a look at what it contains. The case is similar for unboxing videos. The viewer gets the chance of joining the anticipation of taking a look at the package contents for the first time.

Similar to reviews and shopping spree videos, these kinds of videos significantly impact the buying decision of customers and can be quite profitable for brands. This is another aspect with a large possibility for influencer marketing.

## *Educational Videos*

This is separate from how to guides, even though they are both educative. They are both distinct enough to stand separately.

There are some vast channels like National Geographic and TED, which are a part of huge official companies and share the materials of these companies. There are equally lots of other organizations, small and large, that share educational videos on their website.

Another kind of educational video channel places emphasis on offering educational videos for school students and young kids. They try to provide exciting and thought triggering videos for their young viewers.

This is another field which can be classified as continuously profitable. This is because lots of these form of videos attain new viewers yearly and also get repeat viewers.

## Parodies

There are not a lot of parody channels on YouTube. Some are more talented and successful than others. A few of them make the best parodies of movies and others of music videos but often do it professionally.

These are somewhat the most difficult kinds of videos to make. It is straightforward to create a parody that fails to appeal to the audience.

## Pranks

Johnny Knoxville rose to fame using Jackass. It was in a lot of ways the pioneer of all the prank videos on YouTube. They are one of the most shared videos and even spread to other social media outlets as well.

These videos consist of practical jokes on family, friends, and members of the public. Although it is not the most comfortable kind of video for participants to create, these videos are indeed a way for people to rise on social media.

There are some video series where one person plays pranks on another, but the other person gets his vengeance in the subsequent video. There are even prank video series that feature spouses and siblings.

Some pranks may have a bit of controversy, so any brand that wants to associate itself with a prank video must ensure that the values of the pranksters and the company are a great fit.

# Chapter 3: Planning and Developing Your Content Strategy

## Building A Powerful Content Strategy

If you want a successful YouTube channel, it is essential for you to have a great content strategy. Doing things without having a plan would result in you failing even before you begin.

To create a great content strategy, the following tips may be of help. They are:

### *Know What Your Goal Is*

Before you create video content for your YouTube channel, it is crucial for you to create your core objective. There are lots of ways you can use YouTube in developing your brand. But this is only possible if you define the goals of your videos before you produce them.

Do you plan on creating content to grow viewers' awareness of your organization? If yes, be sure that viewers can recognize and recall your brand when they are through watching.

Is your plan to groom the loyalty of your customers? If yes, ensure your viewers will share your video or recommend you after watching.

Is your aim to advertise your product and promote sales? Then ask yourself, will your videos encourage your audience to pay a visit to your website or research the product once they are through watching.

### *Understand your Audience*

You may already possess an accurate sense of your target viewers. However, it is crucial to find out how they act on YouTube. Find out if they utilize their hand-held devices in watching videos or the kind of videos they are viewing.

Look for helpful tools like YouTube Trends Dashboards to aid you in providing solutions to these questions. These tools would give you're the chance to identify the habit of your viewers.

They also let you suitably modify your content.

## Understand Your Brand

If you plan on effectively marketing your brand using your YouTube channel, it is crucial that you define what you stand for. You should also know how you want to present yourself to your viewers.

Define what you want the audience knowing about your services, products, and brand. Also, ensure you pass this information via your content.

## Know Your Competition

Invest time in researching and viewing the videos of your competitors. Doing this will allow you to see the kinds of video content they are creating. What are they successfully and the areas you can improve.

Use this research in getting inspiration for your videos and create a marketing strategy for your YouTube content that makes you stand out. If you don't know where to locate your competitors, try using keywords associated with your organization to search on YouTube. Then check out the videos that are in line with your industry.

### *Identify What Success Looks Like*

Before you can produce amazing branded videos, you need to pinpoint what success for you and your organization looks like. Is a successful video one that urges a ton of user engagement or one that draws in the most views?

You will only be able to develop YouTube content that can meet the needs of your audience the instant you have established what success means to you.

## Why Does Content Strategy Differ With Video

Content strategy is complicated. However, if you break it down to its most straightforward form, you will find out that the most desired result is discoverability.

Irrespective of if it is a specific niche or a broad demographic, you will be contending for their trust and attention.

By fixating over customer queries and becoming the one who answers these questions, your organization will see a fast rise in sales, traffic, and leads. At times, this may not even take weeks.

Videos have become a core aspect of these strategies. Internationally, traffic from online videos will make up for more than 80 percent of all customer internet traffic by the year 2020. Also, searches that relate to; "How To" are rising by 70 percent yearly.

But, videos can be more than tools for education. A video is graphic, and this allows people to make connections emotionally.

You can use videos to reach your viewers continuously and ensure they stay engaged. Videos on Facebook alone have increased by more than 300 percent on the news feeds of everyone.

## The Three Strategies for Video

After you have created a main content strategy, you can begin to split your efforts into the strategies below:

First, you need to **INSPIRE** your viewers using relatable and emotional stories

Next, you have to **EDUCATE** your viewers by using relevant information

Lastly, you need to **ENTERTAIN** your viewers by surprising them. You need to share unique content or make them laugh.

With these, you can go a little further by actually naming each process. Google proposes these kinds of content:

- **Help Content**: what do your viewers actively search for as regards your industry or brand? What can act as your relevant content which you produce every day? These could range from customer service, How-to content, Tutorials on product use, etc.

- **Hub content**: This is the content you regularly develop to offer a fresh perspective on the passion points of your clients.

- **Hero content:** What content do you plan on Pushing to a broad, large audience? What would be your major moment? A brand might have just one of these moments each year, like launching a new product.

Now, let us take a more comprehensive look at these strategies.

### *The Help Strategy*

When your prospective viewers have questions, there is a less likelihood of them picking up the phone. They head to search engines like YouTube or Google, where they input their queries.

Their search may be for things like: "How to Make

Great Videos."

The Help strategy is where you utilize methods of discoverability and SEO. Teach your audience using relevant information, and you will begin to draw in extra viewers to your channel.

Begin with core issues you solve, and regular questions you find people asking about your products. These are core video content individuals always search for actively. By utilizing these sort of videos, asides from educating potential clients, you will also build authority and trust with your viewers.

Some of the most successful titles on YouTube include How To videos, Top AB, and Best of Videos. Take advantage of this and watch your brand and channel grow.

### *Hero Strategy*

This is that video or content that takes lots of time to produce. It should be able to perform so greatly, that you will be able to draw in new viewers and broaden your audience.

This is not so easy, but if you plan correctly, it is attainable. This is the moment you put yourself in the shoes of your ideal viewer and think about things that trigger them. What would they find inspiring?

When you are planning to create this sort of content, imagine it this way: What kind of message can you offer to your audience that would provide them with a new experience?

Send a message loud enough to help them always remember how you made them feel.

### *Hub Strategy*

This is the video content your viewers expect you to offer regularly. This could be each day, weekly, every month or any level of consistency you can manage.

It is just another chance of reinforcing your brand and delighting your customers and prospects.

Most times, you may include this in your educational strategy.

The concept behind this content is to provide content which is relevant and also entertaining frequently. This can be in form or short or long content. Irrespective of what you choose, the aim is to remain consistent and grow your views with time.

## How You Can You Develop The Ideal Video Marketing Strategy?

All of these strategies individually are quite powerful. If you are executing them the right way, you are guaranteed to see a few results. However, take time to observe if you have ideas you can use in these strategies to combine them.

You may observe that your skills are excellent for one or all of these strategies.

## Getting Your Videos to Trend

## What Is A Viral Video?

There is no formal definition of what a viral video means. However, it is any clip on YouTube that gains enormous popularity in a short time. This occurs via sharing via emails, social media, recognized websites among a host of others. But it also happens by attaining views on YouTube's algorithm and search engine.

As stated by YouTuber Nalts, every video that attains more than 5 million views in lower than a week is generally categorized as viral. Previously, the number of views required for a video to be eligible for virility was much lower, but it rose higher as the number of users on YouTube increased.

### *Kinds of Videos That Go Viral*

The fact is there are specific videos which have a higher likelihood of going viral than others. Some of these include:

- **Music Videos**: Over 90 percent of the most-viewed videos on YouTube are music videos. Presently, Despacito by Luis Fonsi is on top of the list with more than 4 billion views.

- **Kid Videos**: The five entries leading the leading 100 lists that are not music videos include Wheels on the Bus, Masha and the Bear among others. All of these are videos meant for children.

- **Funny Falls and Mishaps:** As stated by Dr.William F. Fry, the creator of gelotology which is the science of laughter; it is a natural thing for humans to find it funny when another person falls or experiences a minor misfortune. Obviously, these videos are not funny when they have severe penalties even though videos like that still draw in views from curious individuals.

- **Funny Videos** of Animals: Lots of people love laughter, which is why it is not surprising that videos which feature cute animals often go viral.

- **Unsuitable Videos**: people love to watch shocking videos that challenge the prevailing norms in morality. These videos are not as prevalent on YouTube only because they are banned or only adults are allowed to view them.

- **Videos of Celebrity**: Everything specific celebrities engage in is entertaining to some individual. What this means is that even videos of stars which seem boring, tend to attain numerous views on YouTube. Nonetheless, celebrity fails or fights usually draw in the most attention.

As you must have noticed from the above examples, luck has a significant role to play when it comes to YouTube. What this means is, you will require a lucky break. The sad news is that a typical YouTuber does not get the chance to make videos that will gain virility by themselves.

Rather than depending on luck alone, Vloggers

have to do all they can to ensure their videos gain popularity. Although this is not easy to do, making your videos trend or go viral is entirely possible.

## Tips To Help Your Videos Go Viral

So, how can you make your video go viral? Below are some things you can do to improve the possibility of your videos going viral

### *Optimize Your Videos*

The truth is that a vast part of YouTubers are running their channels as a hobby. They are not experts, and this means that most of them have limited knowledge of online marketing. As a matter of fact, lots of them do not even have an understanding of SEO.

This is where your opportunity comes in. By carrying out appropriate search engine optimization, your videos will have a better ranking on the search results page of YouTube. Also, this will get you more views.

The following are a few ways of optimizing your videos. They include:

- **Optimize Description & Title**

By adding appropriate keywords in video descriptions and titles, you will inform YouTube algorithms about what your content contains. In doing this, you will have the capacity to reveal your videos to users who have an interest in the subject.

For you to properly take advantage of this, you will have to locate the keywords users search for frequently. To do this, you will have to make use of a tool for researching keywords like keywordtool.io.

Another thing to note is to ensure that the descriptions and titles are sensible, even if they have rich keywords.

- **Use Appropriate Tags**

Using the right video tags can give you an edge over your competitors. The reality is that not a lot of vloggers are utilizing tags on their YouTube videos. For those that do, it is not in all of their videos.

You can place keywords of up to 500 characters. So, ensure you select the leading ones. By leading, it means those that are presently popular but have a low level of competition as well.

## Promote On Social Media

Promotion on various platforms is one of the leading ways of getting people to gain interest in your videos. When you post your videos on social media websites like Twitter, Facebook or Instagram, it will be more seamless for you to spread the word as regards them.

## Back-Linking

One of the most crucial factors in SEO is back-linking. This means that the number of links directed towards a particular video has a massive influence on the search engine ranking. But asides from quantity, the quality is equally crucial.

## *Get the Attention of Huge Websites*

Getting the attention of a website with lots of influence can lead you to fame on YouTube. To gauge the possibility of a video getting viral later on, YouTube utilizes an algorithm called the Reference Rank.

If it observes that your video has massive potential of going viral, you will get an email containing a proposal for profit sharing. The algorithm goes through videos with the present view counts lower than 20k. It makes use of a host of criteria to determine the popularity of the video. The most important being if sites with influence have shared the videos.

The more the influence the website that shares your content has, the more the views your videos would attain. For example, the video David After Dentist got posted on Reddit when it has less than 2000 views on YouTube. The count rose to

6 million after just three days!!

The real issue is how you can make these websites learn about your video. Again, the severe competition is an issue. Editors of popular sites don't have adequate time to go through every video on YouTube.

As opposed to hoping someone would see your video, you can solve this by contacting them first. Sadly, this process takes lots of time. To get across to large websites, you need to go step-by-step.

The odds are that the editors on this website won't even come across your video except someone they respect recommends them. That is why it is crucial you make efforts to get an influencer attracted to your video.

### *Develop a Funnel*

You could create the most relatable, entertaining and convincing video worldwide, but if the location you direct your viewers to is not up to standard, you can lose a lot of cash and equally waste lots of time.

If your website does not have a good conversion rate, or if you are nor running search the right way, then you are trying to fill up a basket with water.

### *Getting the Attention of Influencers*

An influencer by definition is a user whose view on specific subject matters to a vast number of individuals or a lesser group with even more significant influence.

As opposed to trying to target the entire audience, it is a great idea to try reaching out to an influencer. He/she would then aid you in spreading around the word of your video. Doing this will ascertain it gets to the appropriate audience which are editors and blog owners of a popular website.

But getting the attention of any influencer is not adequate. You have to make the video appealing to influencers in the same niche as you.

## *How Do You Locate Influencers*

Forbes magazine puts together a list of the leading influencers worldwide annually. These influencers are divided into various categories which include travel, sports, parenting among a range of others. It would be a smart choice to check it out and find out a way to reach out with those individuals.

Typically, reaching out to influencers is via social media. You can be confident that every one of them is active on platforms like Twitter and Facebook. Nonetheless, sending them messages and tweets does not mean you will get a response. In this situation, it may be a smart choice to reach them through their friends. These are other users they see as influential.

Even if you can do this, it's not an assurance that they will like your video. You can only make sure of this if you do all you can when producing the video. After all, the most crucial thing is the content.

## Content Is Crucial

You can invest lots of cash to create awareness for your video. However, you are not going to go viral except the material is excellent. So the first issue you need to fix is how to produce a viral video.

That is why you need to do all you can to make a leading video. You have to cover all the essential parts, beginning from the topic. If the subject of your topic is not trending presently, the possibility is that not lots of people will bother about it.

You also need to make sure that the video visually looks great. It has to be vibrant so that your audience would stay engaged. Lastly, you have to put in a lot of energy and time into editing your videos.

Only after creating a work of art can you hope

your content will go viral.

## How Do I Grow With The Help Of Trending Topics?

Most times, the hardest aspect of creating content is bringing up concepts for new videos. This is the case especially if you don't upload regularly. One thing which leading online video creators share in common is that they have current content.

Irrespective of if it is political news, celebrity talks or huge events, using trends is a sure-fire method of growing your channel.

## How to Find Trends

Except you are living on a mountain, you certainly know about a few trends at least. But to grasp what is happening in the world presently, there are few locations to begin;

### *Facebook And Twitter*

Both of these social networks display topics that

are currently trending in the sidebar. In some situations, you will be able to set it up to focus on a precise country, state or city. Clicking on a topic which is trending will show you the leading posts users on each network are presently talking about.

In most situations, Twitter and Facebook trends get real-time updates. They focus on issues taking place at the very period you are logged in. If you are someone who uploads spontaneously, producing content which focuses on these trends can make you stand out from other YouTubers.

### *Google*

The top location for finding out what individuals are looking for is the location in which they are searching. Google offers an excellent service known as Trends. It highlights what is presently trending and what was trending before.

If you do not find a subject you like that is presently trending, look for what was trending before. There is a high possibility that audiences around the globe are still searching for them.

As opposed to Twitter, Google Trend allows you emphasis on categories you have an interest in to see trending topics on a more precise level. This is ideal if you cover topics like travel, sports, and science.

### *Make Plans In Advance*

There are some trends which come up unexpectedly like current events and news. However, you will be able to predict most of them. If you need your videos to as much attention as it can get, map them out around subjects that can trend later on.

For example:

- The release of a major movie

- The public presentation of a hyped game

- A championship match

- A huge public event

- The season finale of a major TV show

You could plan out using any of the examples above beforehand. Then, you release them when the event takes place. Also, lots of websites list out events coming up. IGN, for example, has a section for the set to be released video games. IMDB also has a similar part for movies.

## Making Use of Trends

Developing content around presently trending subjects can significantly boost your viewership and search visibility. Although these search terms will be seriously competitive, with lots of people carrying out searches daily, you are certainly going to be noticed. As with any recently trending topic, the earlier you take advantage of it, the better your content will do.

### *Remember To Use Meta!*

When the time to upload your recent video,

ensure you add trending keywords in the tags, title, and description. Adding the exact keywords in each of these locations can significantly increase the possibility that your content will be located.

## *Tackling Comebacks*

Even if you covered a topic in the past, you could rejuvenate it if it makes future news later on.

Covering subjects that have the possibility of making a comeback can aid in keeping your viewership great.

## *Engage Your Viewers*

It is one thing to speak about trending topics. However, engaging your viewers can aid your channel in growing further. The more your viewers are engaged, the more the possibility of viewers seeing your video- and the more likelihood of people subscribing.

One easy method of engaging your audience is to

ask questions and inspire subscribing like:

- What is your opinion about ABC? Drop your comments below!!

- Ensure your Subscribe to keep track of Future Releases!!

### *Remember To Share!*

Just like with every trending topic, there is likely to lots of attention on forums and across social media platforms. When you share a video, below are some of the tips that can aid in driving viewership:

- Remember Hashtags; if the subject of your video is trending, add any useful hashtags in your status updates and Tweets.

- Spread your updates all through the day: Do not spam your followers at once. It can be annoying to them.

- Post on forums: it's okay to add your video in threads. But ensure it is significant to the topic. Also, ensure you regulate the number of times you distribute your content.

- Become a member of communities: Lots of social networks like Google+ and Facebook have communities or groups committed to precise subjects. Ensure you join and share any content you may have, but be wary while sharing as no one loves a spammer.

During the period you went through this article, some trends have started, and some have ended. Head out to see what is trending presently and begin making great content.

## How Can My Videos Rank In YouTube's Search Results?

YouTube is one of the biggest platforms as regards having the most numbers of channels, videos, subscribers, audience and followers. It is, for this reason, anyone can search for you when you are on YouTube. However, because there are too many people on YouTube, the primary question which comes up is: How to reach more followers and audience.

YouTube is not complicated. Basically, the more searches and views a video has, it will be moved to the top. Also, the shares and likes of a video have a crucial role to play. This allows the YouTube algorithm to know that a lot of individuals are viewing this content and it is trending.

## How to Get Your Video Ranked On YouTube?

There are numerous ways of getting more likes, subscribers, and views on your video. All of these means your video will get a higher ranking, and more individuals will be able to view it.

There are some easy and authentic ways you can use in getting a better YouTube video ranking. Below are a few of them:

## *Develop Great Video Content*

If you check out the leading YouTube videos, you will observe that the most crucial thing is content. Content is King here. Search by yourself and view the first videos. They will most likely have great content which draws in the attention of the audience, gets more comments, likes, subscribers, and shares.

It is a progression where your content results in more viewers and your audience results in more views which inspire you to create more appealing content. Here, it is essential that you know that great content is always significant now and in the long run.

Additionally, when there is high competition, the quality of your videos is the only thing that can ensure your survival. In essence, irrespective of if you are creating videos that have to do with games, makeup, product reviews or humor, put more effort in the flow, script, facts, quality and information among others. All of these will ensure that you attain your target immediately you hit your audience.

## *Develop New Concepts*

Irrespective of how entertaining it may seem at first, no one will want to keep watching videos they have seen lots of time before. After a while, it begins to lose its appeal, and people start to yearn for new and fresh ideas.

One of the main errors lots of YouTubers make is that they use the same path or concept that aided someone else in attaining fame. Yes, this route may have worked for them, but it does not imply it would also work for you. For one, they could be more experienced in this field while you may not be. Doing this may also result in you missing the opportunity to create videos you are actually great at.

Also, by mimicking a video concept which is already existing, a majority of your viewers will be able, and they will never be drawn to your channel.

This does not imply that you will be unable to go with a specific niche. If there are lots of YouTubers creating gaming related videos, you can equally begin your YouTube gaming channel. However, you need to ensure you are experienced in any niche you choose, you are coming with your style and add a fresh concept which will ensure you stand out from others.

### *Create Short Videos*

Except for movies, nobody will sit to watch a video lasting an hour. Since individuals nowadays have a short attention span.

Also, research has stated that lots of individuals only watch the first minute of a video before heading to the next. That is why you have a very brief time frame to create an impression. It is suggested you begin with short videos and increase the time gradually when you have achieved your target viewers.

Also, make efforts to produce content-rich content and avoid uploading random thoughts as this will only work in distracting your audience.

## *Improve Your SEO*

SEO is crucial in pushing you to the top of the search result. This is the case irrespective of if it is a blog, video, picture or website. It is for this reason you want to enhance your video rankings. You need to make sure you add tags, URL, description, and title using SEO standards. This will aid your videos in organically getting to the top.

## *Grow Your Subscribers*

Another easy and excellent method of improving your video ranking is to get more YouTube subscribers to your channel. They will like, view and share your content which will push you to the top. This is why it is crucial to put in more time attaining adequate subscribers.

# Chapter 4: How to Produce and Film Your Own Videos

## Planning and Outlining: Why Is Planning and Outlining Crucial?

Irrespective of if you are making product reviews or vlogs, planning your videos can aid you in having a better performance on YouTube.

The level of planning you carry out before filming is dependent on you. Some YouTubers do not have enough knowledge of what they plan on saying before they begin recording. However, there are others who script each word.

So irrespective of where you find yourself in this category, below are a few of the top practices for scripting, outlining and planning your YouTube videos.

### *Plan the Initial 15 Seconds*

According to YouTube, the initial 15 seconds of your video is crucial. So, irrespective of how short or long you are planning your shoot to be, ensure you plan the initial 15 seconds of your video.

You specifically want to add a hook which excites people about the content coming up.

Hooks could be anything that seizes attention. But there are a few common kinds of hooks which include:

- A summary of what the video covers

- An appealing visual

- A line which grabs attention

- A teaser for what is about to come up

### *Outline the Main Points*

Nothing is more annoying than shooting a video, only to find out that you did not remember to mention something crucial.

That is why it is essential that you put down a few significant points that are crucial for your video before you begin shooting.

## Pay Attention to Flow

It is not news that viewers of YouTube videos are not exactly patient. That is the reason you need your videos to flow from one point to another quickly.

Except you are naturally skilled, a video with no plan will be filled with lots of pauses that can wreck the drive and flow of your video.

As you make plans for your video, note down how fast you will go from one point to another. Typically, the quicker you move, the better.

Say, you are shooting a Vlog about your trip to Spain, you would want to make a plan for your video, so it does not contain unneeded details.

Your video should cover the essential parts of your trip quickly. This will ensure viewers remain engaged.

## Video Structure; The H.I.C.C

This is a video structure used for outlining

YouTube videos. It is a straightforward yet efficient method.

It works this way:

- **H stands for Hook**

You already know why it is crucial to hook viewers in the initial 15 seconds. But it is something that draws the attention of viewers, so they do not leave.

- **I stands for Intro**

Now that you have the attention of your viewers, it's time to introduce your topic quickly. You can equally show an example or preview of what you will be covering.

- **C stands for Content**

This is the primary content of your video. For a workout video, it is the training itself. For a vlog, it is the activity itself.

- **C stands for Call to Action**

Lastly, you want your video to end using a CTA or call to action to subscribe, like your video, view another of your videos or leave a comment.

### *Shoot For Editing*

A significant aspect of the process of planning has to do with the shoot itself. It consists of the lighting set up, camera angles you will utilize among others.

Shooting for the Edit is a method of planning videos that ensure editing your video is less complicated. It can also lead to an ultimately better video.

Basically, it has to do with planning your shoot around the process of your editing.

In detail, this is how shooting for Editing works;

- Script or outline the material before shooting. It leads in fewer takes to go through and edit.

- Before recording anything, go through 5

seconds or more of test clip to ensure audio, focus and lighting is fine.

- Utilize a clapperboard in keeping up with section and takes. It would also aid in syncing up video and audio.

- For crucial lines, record numerous takes.

## Other Advanced Tips and Strategies

### *Try Utilizing A Teleprompter*

If you script your videos, using a teleprompter can help you save lots of time. Although it takes some time to get around it, the instant you do, you will be able to record videos 25 – 50 percent quicker than reading from your script line by line.

### *Practice*

Engage in a practice session in front of a mirror before the actual shoot. This would result in a smoother shoot. Additionally, practicing offers you the chance to view what won't work and what would before your shoot.

## Learning to Create and Edit YouTube Videos

Developing a YouTube video which is successful has to do with shooting the video as well as editing it into the last production. The process of editing, often known as post-production, aids you in adding numerous shots together into a compelling, unified whole.

Previously, post-production was an expensive process that required costly professional equipment. However, today, you can edit videos using any computer via a low cost or free editing software. You can often compare the quality to what you will see on expensive network news shows and national commercials.

Below are a few steps to help you begin in editing your YouTube video;

## *Choose A Program for Editing Videos*

You utilize the editing program to edit single shots into one video file, which you will be able to upload on YouTube. The editing program also allows you to add graphics, onscreen texts alongside other special effects.

Although it is possible to purchase editing programs like Final Cut Pro from Apple and Adobe Premiere Pro, they can be pricey and complicated to utilize. There are a range of applications that are low-cost or free that can create satisfactory results. If you own a Windows PC, you use the free Movie Maker software from Microsoft.

If you own a Mac, you can use the iMovie free from Apple. All of these programs are great for basic special effects and editing, and they are quite easy to utilize. If you have more advanced requirements, try out Pinnacle Studio, Adobe Premiere Elements alongside Sony Movie Studio Platinum all of which are less than $100. These programs provide more choices for special effects and transitions and create more stylish videos.

### *Edit Your Creation*

Whatever program for editing you decide to go with, piecing together single shots you made into one video can be simple. The objective is to create a video that tells your story effectively.

Majority of the programs for editing provide a timeline view, where you place the individual shots. All of your shots are actually a distinct video file, and you will be placing these video files in your master video timeline. You will be able to shorten or trim any individual shot, move shots about, and delete shots you don't like.

You will then be able to add transitions between shots, like fades to offer you final production a more professional look.

Add Graphics, Text and Other Special Effects

The instant you are editing all your single shots

together into one video, you will be able to enhance it using special effects. For example, most organizations want to add the URL of their website or phone number to the video, which you will be able to do by overlaying that text onscreen. With a majority of the programs for editing, you can accomplish this by adding text layers to your video at specific parts, usually at the start and end of the video.

You can equally superimpose images and other graphics, possibly to display a product package while other actions are occurring onscreen. Other examples of special effects consist of sepia tone, split-screen and soft focus. Additionally, you will be able to add music in the background which could either be your own music or those offered by the editing program. You don't have to be an expert to add these special effects, as a majority of these programs provide you with step-by-step guidance through these functions.

As tempting as it might be to utilize many of these special effects, it's best not to go overboard.

You don't want to draw attention away from your important message with onscreen graphics and other elegant effects. They should aid in telling your story, not cause a hindrance.

### *Select the Appropriate File Format*

When you are through editing your video, you will be able to produce a final video file which you can upload to YouTube and other websites for sharing videos. YouTube supports a majority of the critical file formats, so you are safe irrespective of the one you select. MP4, AVI or WMA formats are recommended options which lots of the main video editing programs support.

When editing your video, ensure you are utilizing a widescreen format of 16:9 ratio, which is generally expected by users. And irrespective of the file format you go with, render your file in either 1080i or 720p. Even if your audience views your video in a format with lower-resolution on their computers, you want to begin with the pick resolution possible in the main file.

Additionally, some viewers will see your videos on huge screens, HD TVs, so you don't want to offer them a version with lower-resolution.

## *Developing Ideas for Your Videos*

YouTube video ideas can come from any location. Search for inspiration in your life, and be sure to seek out opinions from loved ones, friends, employees, coworkers, clients and customers. You will also want to devote time checking out YouTube by watching various kinds of videos that other individuals and companies have created.

The main ideas for videos that you churn-out should be unique and trigger excitement in you alongside your target audience. They need to be interesting, original, thought-provoking, creative and entertaining simultaneously. They should also be relevant to your target audience. One way of starting your search for concepts is to find out what the competition is doing already, and then determine how you can do it differently or better in your videos.

There is already a large amount of content on YouTube, so creating your original concept can be quite tedious. Instead, focus on methods of making your ideas stand out from what is already available. Don't be scared to go with the trend and get your inspiration from popular videos, so long as you are willing and able to add an original, unique and convincing twist. If you decide to utilize other videos to get inspiration, ensure you are not violating the copyrights, trademarks or properties of anyone else when you create your videos.

Immediately you have a basic idea about what your overall objectives are for YouTube, outlined your core message and defined your audience, and you need to start brainstorming ideas for individual videos.

Begin by deciding what you want to say. Then, depending on your video production equipment, skills and abilities, consider the best methods of presenting that content.

For every possible idea you come up with, answer the following:

- Does my concept go with what I want to achieve on YouTube?

- Will my idea and planned method be appealing to my target audience?

- Do I possess the knowledge, skill and appropriate equipment to create the video I am planning and do it properly?

- Can I produce a video that suits my budget, without compromising the quality of production?

- What reaction do I want from my audience? What will be my call to action?

- How do I predict the audience will respond to the video?

- Will viewing this video lure the viewer to watch other videos I have on my YouTube channel, to somehow reach out to me or my organization, or to purchase my service/product, if relevant?

- When anyone is viewing the video or the instant it is through, will they have the drive to give an excellent rating, like the video, share the video with their friends online using other social media outlets or post a great comment?

- Does the video, its call to action, its message and its overall approach go with what I am doing already for my company or myself in other online outlets?

During the whole pre-production stage, and then during post-production, ask yourself the questions above repeatedly to ensure you are on point.

As you answer every one of these questions, you will often realize the necessity to tweak or fine-tune your initial ideas to change them into something that is more on-target or relevant with your message, overall goals, and call to action. At the same period you are accessing your concept, consider original, off-beat and creative methods of presenting your content in a unique or fun way.

Then before you invest too much cash or time as you go further in the pre-production stage, present your concept to other individuals who know you, your organization, target audience, and your online objective.

Sharing ideas with other creative individuals you trust will aid you in considering things from various perspectives. These could affect how the audience accepts or perceives your videos.

If your objective is to create a YouTube channel and fill it with new videos frequently, during the initial stage of generating ideas, create a list of outline ideas for your initial five videos or so. Then, as you think of new concepts in the future, ensure you put them down so you can refer to them at a later date.

Ensure that what you plan on doing with your

YouTube channel is consistent and sustainable with your online business reputation, brand, and general business model. For example, you may have amazing concepts for your initial videos, but how do you plan on maintaining and growing your audience going forward? Figuring all of these will ensure you have a successful channel.

## How to Overcome Your Fear of the Camera?

Dry mouth, butterflies and even slight nausea are all signs that you are not comfortable in front of a camera. This is a very common experience for lots of individuals. In fact, for some, it has become a normal occurrence.

But it does not have to be so. If you plan on creating a successful YouTube channel, you need to be comfortable in front of a camera.

Here, we will be looking at a few tips for dealing with your fear of the camera to aid you in confidently facing the camera.

## *Practice Frequently and Early*

If you are sure you are not doing the wrong thing, you won't be that uncomfortable. When you learn by heart all you have to do or say in every take, you will eradicate the risk of missing something if you get anxious.

At times, it may not even have to do with remembering your cues or lines. It can also be the process of hitting record or setting up your camera. Make time to practice this process, even if you are messing around. It will begin to seem less intimidating with time.

## *Be Ready For Errors*

Even if you have rehearsed numerous times, you may still get stuck a few times immediately the camera begins rolling. Plan in advance, and brainstorm ways to free your mind in case.

For example, you could put down notes which you can display behind the camera to aid in jogging your memory if you get frozen. You could also create mnemonic devices to assist you in remembering.

## Film Numerous Takes

The most natural video can enjoy numerous takes. At times, the words come out a bit clearer after trying it again. You may be able to make the lighting a little better, or there may be a silly mistake that you have to hide using a smart edit.

Filming many takes means there is not as much pressure on any individual shot to attain perfection. If you develop this approach into your filming plan, it will aid you in relaxing knowing you will be able to try it again in some minutes.

## Take Deep Breaths

A precise kind of breathing technique can aid you in focusing your mind and distressing your body. Another important aspect is that it can help your voice in going down numerous octaves if you are already nervous and are a bit squeaky.

It is known as belly breathing. You begin by deeply inhaling via your nose, allowing your stomach naturally expand as your lungs take in air. Release the air from your lungs slowly, emulating the time it required for you to fill them up.

Sometimes it is helpful if you do a countdown as you inhale and exhale. Continue this process until you begin to feel relaxed. It is crucial not to breathe in as fast as normal when utilizing this technique. Because you will be taking in higher levels of oxygen than usual, your regular breathing pace could result in your yawning or feeling light-headed. Ensure you take it slow, and you would be alright.

Belly breathing aids in balancing the carbon dioxide and oxygen levels in your blood. This functions by eradicating itchy sensations in your extremities, sweaty palms and other stress symptoms. Try it for a while and note the huge difference it can make.

It also passes a sign to your brain that you should relax. This kind of deep breathing is linked to natural states of relaxation. It also informs your brain that it is okay to calm down.

### Study Experts

When next you turn on your television, make it an objective to see how individuals on screen perform. Are they standing or seated? How fast do they speak? Where do they stare at when speaking? What kind of gestures do they utilize?

All of this information can inform how you perform when facing a camera. It may also aid you in creating your persona or camera, or to mimic a particular person.

### Take Public Speaking Classes

Portraying confidence is crucial in public speaking. Getting used to standing in front of a crown can significantly aid with your camera appearance.

Universities or high schools often have classes you can take for free. Taking just one seminar that has to do with public speaking could offer you some tips you can utilize on camera.

### *Turn It into A Habit*

If you make videos sparingly, it would not be so easy to deal with your fears as opposed to if you do it every other day. We are often scared of the unknown.

It is not compulsory that it has to be a professional or polished production. There are lots of ways you can work video into your daily life. Try to create fun videos on Instagram, Snapchat or Facebook and share with your loved ones and friends. Do a live broadcast and go with a video call as opposed to a regular phone call.

Change your presentation into a video. The more you make videos, the less scary it will be along the line.

### *Do A Video Challenge*

To aid you in dealing with your nervousness and freezing, obligate yourself to create one video daily, weekly or each month. Choose a theme, add it to your schedule and pick the time to deal with it in advance.

During the period of this challenge, you are probably going to make errors, and that is perfectly okay. This is the whole concept. Learning from mistakes will aid you in growing your confidence that you will do it correctly the next time.

### *Put On Your Best Outfit*

There is a saying that goes thus; if you look great, you will feel great. It is not a problem if your best gear seems unusual. After all, for numerous years TV personalities have worn amazing outfits.

However, not that there is a clear distinction between unusual and inappropriate. So ensure your clothes are free of wrinkles and clean. Stay away from shiny accessories, stripes, and little patterns, as they can result in visual problems on camera. Noisy jewelry is also not an option as it can impede the audio.

## Offer To Help With Other Projects

Do you have any friends creating a video? Or a local video studio that requires talent? Or is there a play nearby?

Volunteer your time to assist others with video jobs. You will learn more every time you partake in a shoot. Even when not on camera, you can still learn some things when you participate in a production.

## Head Behind the Camera

Coaching another person on camera may let you feel less anxious in front of it. Seeing it from another side can aid you in gaining perspective on what works and what does not.

## *Make Your Gaze Focused*

Lots of people deal with the issue of not knowing where to stare at when on camera. The answer is that it is dependent on the kind of video you are creating.

If you are making a live action video, you need to avoid staring into the lens except it is scripted.

For an interview, the subject has to face the individual interviewing them. You can set up the camera to the interviewer side. You can also utilize numerous cameras to get both aspects of the conversation. Irrespective of what the case is, the subject should stare at the interviewer as opposed to the camera

If you are making a talking head video, you need to stare straight into the camera. If this is too difficult for you, you can try staring a little above the camera, or the individual behind the camera.

Keeping a firm gaze will let you portray confidence on camera, irrespective of if you are feeling it or not.

### *Utilize Biofeedback*

Belly breathing is not the only method of telling your body to relax. You can also utilize gentle stretching and correct posture to decrease tension.

For example, if you observe yourself tightly crossing your legs and arms, fidgeting or wringing your hands, all you are doing is strengthening your nervous situation.

If you are standing, it is a good idea to loosely clasp your hands in front of your body while having your elbows bent. Ensure your feet are a comfortable distance away from each other. Moving too much or swaying may result in you falling out of frame, so make an effort to keep your torso in one place. It is okay to slant your head, move your weight from one side to another or express yourself by moving your arms instead.

In between sessions, walk about, roll your

shoulders, and gently stretch your arms to ensure it does not get stiff.

## What Essential Equipment Do You Require to Begin a YouTube Channel?

If you have plans to become a YouTuber officially, there are a lot of things you need to have in place. The most crucial is your video equipment.

Producing quality videos is not without its difficulties. The great news is that you don't require lots of technical knowledge to create the form of content viewers would love watching. All you need is the appropriate equipment.

If you have genuinely fantastic content, a unique and great personality, you will most likely do fine using a smartphone alone. However, note that YouTube is now quite competitive, and a starter, it is crucial to try harder when it comes to your video visual quality to make sure you attain views and subscribers.

Lots of popular YouTubers utilize a broad range of sophisticated equipment for video production. There are some who even get the services of professional camera operators and video editors to create their videos. However, you don't have to go that far.

Below are a few of the necessary equipment for video production you will require to begin your YouTube channel. They are:

- Camera

- Tripod

- Lighting

- Microphone

- Video Editing Software

### *Camera*

This is obviously the most crucial piece of equipment to own. But before rushing to purchase the first camera, you see at the camera store, note that it is not compulsory for you to purchase the costliest DSLR you find. You can use almost anything that can record videos of high quality. At least 1080p.

Quality webcams or camcorder would do fine if you are just beginning. However, mirrorless cameras and DSLRs are great investments when you want to upgrade. Remember that the kind of camera you should buy is greatly dependent on the sort of content you desire to produce on YouTube. You can select from any of the following types of cameras. They are:

- **Camcorder**

Camcorders are an ideal option for producing content on YouTube because they are created explicitly for recording videos. Also, recent camcorders are lightweight, quite affordable, portable and constructed to deal with almost all kinds of shooting situations. You can utilize them when shooting a video in your home or Vlogging on the move.

- **Webcam**

If you want a video camera which is affordable with plug and play functionality, this is a great choice. It is especially ideal for those who have to record in front of their laptops like gamers on YouTube. Webcams also ensure it is less stressful to live stream since you can connect them directly to your computer.

- **Action Camera**

Action cameras are recognized as the most versatile and portable kinds of camera. They are ideal for videographers and photographers who desire to capture the first-person Point of Views of their extreme sports adventures or travels. Irrespective of their little size, lots of them can develop videos of the highest quality you can find today. It is for this reason lots of YouTubers utilize these cameras for the durability and video quality they provide.

- **Mirrorless Camera**

These have become the most recognized kinds of cameras for both photographers and video creators. This is due to their capacity to shoot videos similar to DSLR but with a body which is quite smaller and lighter.

Although this camera can be utilized for recording videos in your home, they are also ideal if you require a camera for video blogging while moving about or walking.

The most popular choice among YouTubers are DSLRs due to the high-quality results they provide. The way they adapt to low light scenarios and refined video recording quality are just some of the primary reasons they are a fantastic choice for developing content on YouTube.

Though they don't come cheap, DSLRs provide value for money spent if you desire to be serious about photography and videography.

## *External Microphone*

Don't forget that the quality of your audio has to match your video. Even if you shoot videos using 4K footage, if your audio is terrible, you will have issues keeping viewers engaged. Camera microphones in laptops also have awful audio quality because they can't record or eradicate ambient sounds efficiently. So a quality microphone is the next crucial tool you need to own if you want to make great YouTube videos.

However, before rushing out to buy the first one, you find, ensure you learn about the various kinds of microphones to make sure you are getting the perfect one for your requirements.

Below are a few of the various kinds;

- **USB Microphones**

These microphones grew from being unknown to one of the best choices for YouTubers. These kinds of mics have made their name due to the sound quality they offer, the ease of usage alongside how affordable and versatile they are.

- **Condenser Microphone**

This form of microphone does not require a pre-amp and supports self-monitoring using the headphone jack built into it with volume control. It also provides you with mix control which lets you blend the audio of your microphone with pre-recorded audio. Most condenser microphones of high quality come with extended frequency response. It makes them great for home recording and recording vocals for podcasting.

- **Shotgun Microphones**

Shotgun microphones are a popular, high-quality choice for recording videos using a portable, professional camera. These microphones are already produced with shock mounts that aid in minimizing noise that arise from vibrations around the microphone.

Another significant feature is its capacity to focus

on catching clear vocals and sounds straight in front of it. For this reason, it does not capture too many ambient sounds behind the mic and on the sides even when you are recording outside.

- **Lapel Microphone**

This is also called a lapel mic. It is a wireless mic and can be clipped inconspicuously onto your belt or clothes. It comes alongside a set that consists of a transmitter, where you connect the lapel. It also has a receiver which can capture the signal the transmitter sends out, even from a great range.

### *Gimbal Stabilizer or Tripod*

Having footage which is not steady is not ideal for the production of professional videos. It can also make your viewers dizzy or divert their attention. Gimbal stabilizers and tripods are excellent tools for stabilizing your videos and photos.

Depending on how you want to record your

video, you can pick any of them to enhance your YouTube videos production value.

- **Tripod**

A tripod is a more budget-friendly option. Lots of them don't cost more than $100 and still offer great results, depending on how much your camera setup weighs.

But, it is still ideal to purchase a more reliable and durable tripod that can stand the test of time. It is also ideal as it helps in ensuring the security of your camera equipment.

- **Gimbal Stabilizer**

Irrespective of how you try to hold your camera steady, shooting with your hands will produce jarring and shaky videos. Gimbal stabilizers are created using weights or motors to balance your camera carefully and make your videos smoother, even if you dart during a shoot.

It is a really great option for YouTubers utilizing lightweight and portable cameras like GoPros and are continuously on the move.

## *Lighting*

Lighting equipment is a necessity if your primary areas of recording are in dimly lit environments and indoors. And even if you are doing your shoot where there is adequate ambient light, lighting equipment can aid in modifying the mood. It can also help you in evening out your setup's brightness.

Below are the forms of lighting equipment you can utilize when recording your videos for YouTube.

- **Softbox**

These can mimic soft, natural lighting from a window. It is as a result of the white diffusion panel which aids in defusing and minimizing the intensity of direct, harsh light.

This kind of lighting equipment is great if you want additional lighting that does not create harsh shadows for your subject or scene.

- **Umbrella Light**

Umbrella lights are a portable and budget-friendly solution for video producers who require soft lighting. In comparison to softboxes, umbrellas produce lighting which is more controlled as it reflects light from the internal silver layer of the umbrella.

It does not come with a diffusing sheet. However, it can cover a vast portion of space. They are great for on-location shoots and backdrops.

- **Ring Light**

Ring lights are a leading choice among bloggers. Its ring shape radiates light which goes all around the subject. When this occurs, it eradicates shadows from all directions. It makes anyone look more appealing in front of a camera.

It is the reason a lot of beauty, and makeup vloggers often use it because they can light up the face beautifully. They can also eradicate shadows that tend to make blemishes noticeable.

- **On-Camera Lighting**

On-camera lights offer constant lighting. Also, you can mount them on cameras. They can be an ideal option for recording specific kinds of videos like documentary channels, wedding videos or content on YouTube that has to do with individuals and dimly-lit areas.

### *Video Editing Software*

The instant you have attained all the hardware you require, it is also essential that you locate a great video editing software. YouTube offers its video editor, but it would be nice to have your software. This will ensure you have less limitation when it has to do with modifying your videos the way you want.

For videographers in general, Adobe Premiere Elements 18 is a favorite option. It comes from the leading industry leader in software for video editing. It offers tools which are very usable and a broad range of options for editing. Some of these include freeze frames, animations, video trimming, and bounce back effects among others. All of these offer your professional video quality your viewers would love and likely probably subscribe to your channel on YouTube for.

# Chapter 5: Improving Your Video Production

Without a doubt, video content works. It is not really important who creates it, or the goal the individual is. It is just something that works. However, it does not imply that it works every time for everyone. It does not. Similar to any other thing, it requires some know-how and skill. But a few tips can be helpful.

Here, we will be taking a look at some of the easiest and best ways of enhancing your video production.

### *Spell Out What Role the Video Aims to Serve*

Before you make any videos or important decisions, it is crucial that you spell out what you want your video to achieve. You should also determine how it goes with your entire plan. Ensure you are as concise and precise as possible. It will only aid in keeping everyone working towards the same time.

Also, it will save you lots of time in the future. You won't try to do everything simultaneously. You will also have a better understanding of how to gauge your content's performance.

### *Make Plans for Both Silence and Sound*

There are numerous platforms where you can upload your videos. From every possible social media outlet to email, your website among others, you have a variety of options. That is why it is not a bad idea to try producing videos that viewers can understand sound with or without sound.

Irrespective of if this means utilizing graphics, subtitles or captions, or telling your story in a more visual manner, the idea is that you should consider the likelihood of your audience viewing your videos without sound while developing them. It is one of the best methods of enhancing the possibility of your contents been seen.

## *Think From Your Mind*

Lots of marketers, video makers, and brands waste lots of time pretending to be what they are mot with their videos. They see something that works for someone else and believe it can work for them. But the issue is that the content was created by another person, and it probably only worked because the video was in line with their mission and destiny.

That is why it is crucial to let your own attitude and style, alongside your specific goals, decide the forms of videos you produce. This will ensure videos are more true to your person and have more originality.

## *Make Adjustments Based on Feedback and Results*

Another error lots of video creators tend to make is not seeing the signs. Instead, they hold on to the last minute because they feel their plan is still going to succeed. But, numbers hardly lie.

So, if you are not really getting the positive results you expected, and you are getting feedback from your audience, then don't be scared of adjusting accordingly. Monitoring performance and paying attention to your audience are very vital pieces for success.

## *Maintain Some Consistency*

While a significant aspect of producing videos that are unique is the willingness to tell your stories using new methods, it is also crucial that they are still connected in some manner. Irrespective of the specific goal or style of the video, there should still be something universal that people would know you for. You must always remember this because if you don't, your viewers won't either.

So, don't just attach your banner to the end of the video. Consider some aspects like your overall tone and manner and the types of stories you tell.

## *Locate the Right Crew*

Possibly the fasted method of instantly enhancing your video production plan is to locate the ideal crew for the kinds of videos you produce. This not only has to do with finding skillful, experienced and talented individuals with a great work portfolio. But it also means locating the right individuals for the job.

These do not necessarily mean picking the crew with the most talents. It means choosing people that have personalities and styles similar to yours. This way, you will have the capacity to grasp your voice and identity alongside the concept of your video.

## How Can I Make Videos That Are Better Looking And Sounding?

Having a great video idea is one thing. But if you edit your video sloppily, it would leave you with a final product your viewers would find unbearable to watch nor engage.

Here, we will be taking a look at some great tips for editing your videos to be more engaging.

### *Select the Ideal Camera Angles for Every Moment*

As you go through your recording, your objective is to balance the intention of the speaker to what the web viewers expect. Determine where the viewers would want to be viewing at various points during the shoot if they were also in the room. This will aid you in selecting the perfect camera angle for reconstructing every moment.

By considering this, you will also be selecting angles that aid the speaker in telling his/her story better.

### *Lose the Script*

Nothing feels less authentic than a person who reads from a prepared text or sounds like they memorized a script in detail. When you try recalling each word, your delivery slows down and becomes more robotic and stiff.

Viewers prefer speakers who appear more personable, conversational and natural. A better idea is to memorize your introductory and concluding line. Then read the remainder without learning it word-for-word.

## Keep Your Posture Open

A stiff performance means movement is minimal. For example, if you place both hands tightly to your side or you cross your arms in front of your body. You need to actually loosen up.

Don't be scared to make use of your hands, especially if you are in natural conversations. Leave your palms turned up as much as you can. Don't obstruct your body. An open posture portrays comfort and confidence.

## Work on Your Presence on Camera

If you feature in your professional videos, how you carry yourself while on camera has a massive effect on how your content looks. Seeming fidgety, uncomfortable or nervous will distract your audience from the message you are trying to pass across.

The great news is that this is what you can work on with practice. If you are not a natural with amazing camera presence, below are some of the significant things to focus on when filming yourself.

- Utilize open, calm body language. Stand upright. If you have poor posture, it is instantly noticeable on camera. Relax your muscles and back while taking deep breathes. Do not cross your arms as this makes you seem closed-off.

- Smile, especially at the start of your video. It makes a massive difference in how friendly you seem.

- Slightly slow down when you speak and try to articulate clearly. Speak through your diaphragm as opposed to your throat.

- If you feel fidgety, occupy your hands with

a prop. For instance, writing on a whiteboard can provide you with something to focus on asides the camera.

- Practice continuously. Go through footages of yourself and note the areas you need improvement. Then after practice try consciously to work on those areas.

## Shoot From Many Angles

An excellent method of adding visual interest to your videos is to cut from one angle to another. It is a great strategy especially if you are creating a product demo, how-to video or other kinds of videos that portray you carrying out an activity as opposed to you just speaking alone.

Shoot lots of B-roll footage for all videos. This ensures you have the opportunity of utilizing it later if you desire.

A great tip is when changing perspectives, shift by 45 degrees at least. Fewer shifts in perspective don't actually produce the effect you intend. They just seem shaky to the viewers.

### *Prioritize Clear, Crisp Audio*

The quality of your audio can be more crucial than the quality of your professional video. Lots of people would choose to watch a video you do not shoot in HD or that is even a bit grainy, so long as every other thing about it is excellent.

However, indistinct, fuzzy audio is usually adequate to make anyone head back within seconds of beginning a video. Because sound is crucial, a great microphone should be the first thing you should purchase. Get an affordable one. For less than $200, you should be able to find one that is durable and performs quite well. There are also some great options if your budget is tight.

Capture clear audio by placing your microphone as close as it can get to the subject. You may want to utilize a pop filter to get rid of crackles and blips on the completed recording. Note any noise at the background your microphone may be picking also.

Tuning out stuff like birds, traffic, and noise the wind makes is not difficult. However, these sounds would be noticeable in your recording.

### *Avoid Unstable Footage.*

Shaky footage will make any footage seem like a home movie. What is more, it can also make your audience feel uneasy. It is not easy to be completely steady when holding a camera, so ensure you don't hold the camera at all if this is possible. A better option is to utilize a tripod or place your camera on a solid surface.

Immediately you have set up your camera, make efforts not to move except you need to. Continuously panning around can consistently make the video seem unprofessional. As opposed to moving the camera if you need to change your perspective, it's a better choice to cut from a shot to another.

If despite your best efforts, you end up with a shaky video, software for video stabilization can aid in fixing it. Some cameras also come with in-built stabilization that you can utilize while filming. Reducing the speed of your footage can also assist in hiding the shakiness.

### *Ensure your Background is Clean*

Be thoughtful about the background you utilize for filming. Noting looks more armature than a background which is distracting or messy. An easy method of getting your video a professional look is to use an environment with a solid color.

A bedsheet, wall or a large sheet of backdrop paper are all great choices. Ensure your object stands a few feet away from the backdrop, so there are no shadows cast on it.

Shooting a video in an environment which is professional is a great idea. Ensure you don't film where there is a reflective surface close by. This is because having some form of light source behind your subject can result in the subject looking shadowy and dark.

## *Do Not Edit Excessively*

It can be more fun to try out a range of effects when you are editing your videos but don't over-do this. A clean, simple style of editing has a more professional look.

Some things to ensure you do during the stage of editing include:

- Utilize noise cancelation to clear up any noise at the background

- Adjust the lighting a bit if you have to

- Remove awkward silences and pauses

- Add transitions and background music

Another great tip is, if you make cuts from one scene to another in your video, do it when there is no movement in both cuts. This is more natural and smoother than moving from one scene where nothing is going on to another.

The more professional your videos seem, the more benefit it will offer your rand. And, although making videos which are professional looking does require a bit of know-how and practice, it is not something you have to study for years, neither is it magic.

With these tips above you will be able to take your video quality up a notch.

## Basic Editing Tips

Although the tips below don't tell you exactly how to edit your video clips, they can aid in halving the time you spend in editing and aid you in producing better final results.

### *Select the Appropriate Software*

The initial step in enhancing the process of your video editing is to select the appropriate software for you. They usually provide all you require to carry out standard video edits, but you may choose one over another for their digital interference, usability, and features.

The idea here is to select what works for your style of editing and yourself as opposed to choosing the most recent program for editing videos available.

Top options include:

- Avid Media Composer

- Premiere Pro

- After Effects

- DaVinci Resolve

If you want options that are not as popular but still capable, you could want to try out Sony Vegas or Lightworks.

### *Utilize A Quick Computer*

Irrespective of the model or brand you desire, you can choose it so long as it has the speed to store massive files. It should also let you focus on your editing work without the need to deal with slow rendering.

It is undoubtedly a good idea to invest in an SSD or faster storage drive. This lets you access your software and files faster. It also speeds up your export, rendering and loading time. You can do other things to reduce your editing time significantly which include increasing the RAM of your computer. You need no less than 8GB if you plan on doing a professional job. You also need to attain the ideal processor and video card for the editing software you use.

### *Edit for a Story*

One thing you should not forget is to your creative objective which is to tell a fantastic story. Go past the basics like correcting the arrangement of your clips and cutting off unnecessary footage. Take the time to ensure your video is dramatically compelling and aesthetically pleasing to trigger the appropriate emotions and pass out your intended message effectively. Utilize your technical and practical know how to attain this as opposed to just including a range of effects to get your audience impressed.

You can just go along with the storyboard utilized while filming. But there may be periods when you will make the decision to make changes on the spot to the effects, scene transitions and other elements of editing to enhance the story.

### *Sustain A Workflow Which Is Efficient*

Even while utilizing a high-speed computer and great editing software, you will also have to be organized and systematic if you want to become a more effective editor. One method of enhancing your workflow is to organize your files and projects you can utilize many times.

Create folders for your images, footages, projects, audio files and graphics where you can also develop more folders and subsections. Another means in which you can work quicker is to utilize external hard drives to store your footage. This allows you free up memory on your computer.

A great idea is to select hard drives you can connect using Thunderbolt or USB 3.0 for quicker transfer of files. You may also want to allocate your RAM, so you have more to use for editing. You can also purchase a gaming mouse that lets you set precise functions for editing on its buttons.

### *Make Use of Keyboard Shortcuts*

When it comes to buttons, note that the majority of the programs for editing let you utilize keyboard shortcuts to carry out a host of editing functions in-app. Feel free to memorize, review and customize the diverse range of shortcuts for software programs like Final Cut Pro, Media Composer, Premiere Pro and Adobe After Effects among others.

If you are okay investing a little cash, a less complicated option would be to buy an editing keyboard. This kind of keyboard already comes with shortcut icons. They are usually specific to software, so you don't have to bother about issues with compatibility.

### *Understand Crucial Terms*

The industry for video editing will need you to interact with other video clients or editors. It means you will need to learn lots of jargon. If you have not come across them before, it can be impossible to figure out some of the terms utilized in editing videos without carrying out any research.

This is why it is essential you learn them beforehand. Some of the basic concepts consist of:

- **Jump Cuts**: Removing parts to skip predictable and boring moments and maintain visual interest.

- **Cutaways**: inputting pieces of transitions that done consist of the main action or action to view the surrounding environment, adds meaning to the scene, sets the mood or helps with dramatic tension.

- **L Cut**: Video comes before the audio.

- **J Cut**: Audio comes before the video.

- **Montage**: Order of clips which show how time passes. It is usually for character development or transformation.

- **Cutting on Action**: making cuts when the subject is on motion instead of after every movement to develop a scene which is more fluid and exciting.

- **Match Cut:** cutting two scenes or shots which are visually similar together.

These are only some of them. There are lots of other terms and cuts to learn. All you have to do is to take some time to do your research and read.

Bennie Sloan

## *Carry Out Color Correction on Your Clips*

Color is a core element of design that you can manipulate to draw out specific emotions, highlight a particular subject and set the atmosphere or mood of your scene. The great news is, the editing programs today offer you lots of options for color editing which were formerly possible just with pictures.

Lots of editors do two major things which are:

- Color grading: to offer your video a distinct look

- Color correction: To ensure you have consistent colors in your footage in every scene

Both are crucial when you want a majority of your scenes to look as genuine as they can. They are also vital in differentiating specific scenes from others, like when you utilize presets like monochrome or sepia on flashback scenes.

## *Pick Great Music*

Don't just place emphasis on the visuals. It has to be as great as your music. If you are creating a video with some drama, for example, you will desire just the appropriate instrumental or song to make crucial moments like where you want to urge specific feelings in your viewers more efficient.

But before you even consider utilizing any kind of music, don't forget that the most secure option is to attain music from a music provider offering royalty free music. You may be able to get some free music, but the top audio usually costs a decent amount.

## *Include Graphics and Text*

Depending on the kind of video you are trying to create, you may have to add extra text apart from the basic. You will also want it to stay simple. However, if you need to embed flashy graphics, you can produce them with the help of your editing software.

Adobe After Effects is a common choice for developing some of the leading motion graphics. If you don't know how to make yours yourself, you can always head to RocketStock to attain ready-made After Effects templates.

### *Utilize Web Versions for Exporting*

The instant you are through with your video and ready for exporting, most editors naturally want to export it using the largest video resolution available. This is an excellent choice if you're going to play in ultra HD screens or cinemas. But if you plan on using it online, you need to send out high-quality, smaller versions.

When you want to export for the web, the objective is to produce a file that preserves its high quality while ensuring it is not too large to upload and view online. If you are not certain about the export settings to utilize, it is not an issue. Websites like Facebook and YouTube all come with suggested export settings.

# Chapter 6: Promoting Your Channel

After producing a video, if you fail to promote it correctly, you are likely going to fail. Video marketing has been growing in popularity over the years, and more brands are beginning to exploit its benefits.

And while recognized websites like Instagram, Facebook, Twitter, and Snap Chat are great locations to invest, YouTube is still a leader in the space, with over millions of people viewing videos on the platform daily.

Often categorized as the second biggest search engine in the globe, YouTube can aid your content in quickly been found. It also ensures your content has lots of engagement if you know what to do.

If you are in search of ways to promote your channel and grow it, below are a few things to try out.

### *Develop Videos Around One Topic/Keyword*

Developing your video around a single keyword or topic is one of the top ways of getting the traffic you desire. It is also great for growing your audience. Lots of individuals do not know about SEO practices and ignore this step. However, it is essential if you need your videos to attain the peak number of viewers.

As we have covered in earlier chapters, using a keyword tool like KeywordTool.io which is YouTube specific to search for the keywords seared the most in the niche you are aiming to target.

It is crucial to choose your keyword before you even develop your video content. This is because it aids you in creating the best information relating to that precise subject. It is also helpful if you remember to add the keyword all around your content naturally, so YouTube can pick it up when you add closed captions.

The instant you have selected your keywords, search for videos that are presently ranking for that topic to ensure you are in the right direction as regards your intention. Also, remember to optimize your descriptions and channels.

Regardless of well-known myths, videos with the most success on YouTube are basically not more than 5 minutes. So, don't believe you need to write a novel or make a movie, Leave it sweet and short.

### *Reformat Prior Quality Content*

The easiest method of promoting and growing your channel is to develop amazing content. But you do not have to always generate the material from the start. You can build some of your leading videos from useful, valuable, actionable and engaging content you have created before.

Lots of individuals head to YouTube to locate how-to tutorials and find solutions to issues they are dealing with, so content that helps in solving issues are ideal options. Check out the guides, blogs and other successful pieces you have presently and think about how to transform them into amazing videos.

### *Provide Your Videos with An Appealing Title*

When people search for videos on YouTube, the two significant elements that will draw their attention is the video title and thumbnail.

The title is the initial thing a person reads when they locate your video. If you want to learn how to promote your channel on YouTube, you need to have the capacity to write exciting and engaging titles for all your videos.

Below are some tips for writing amazing titles:

- Shorten it: Don't let your titles have a length of more than 70 characters. Google will shorten anything more than this in search results.

- Add keywords: The title of the video is one of the top locations where keywords are useful. Utilize primary keywords in writing a brief but helpful title.

- Be compelling: Write a title that is attention-grabbing, catchy and descriptive. Place keywords in the opening half of the title to offer a perfect insight into the topic of the video. But also make efforts to share your passion for the topic at hand.

- Stay away from clickbait: This is a territory you need to stay away from. Clickbait titles are fundamentally misleading or over-sensationalized statements used to spur curiosity. Utilizing clickbait can be detrimental to your brand and wear down the trust between you and your audience. People may be fascinated enough to click the video, but they are probably going to quickly leave if your content does not do what it offers. This will lead to fewer retention rates and watch times which is a huge red flag for YouTube.

## *Utilize Compelling and Attractive Thumbnails*

YouTube thumbnails have a significant influence on if a potential viewer goes through your video. The thumbnail and title work hand in hand to attract fans, build anticipation and ensure your videos have more appeal to your target audience.

Developing custom thumbnail offers lots of benefits to your videos. Some of these are:

- Improves your channel with a more polished and professional look.

- Enhance your videos click-through rate.

- Draw attention from the appropriate audience and earn a better rate of retention. An excellent thumbnail will give individuals an idea about your topic. For this reason, people who click your video have a higher likelihood of finishing the video.

Find out how you can promote your channel on YouTube using custom-made video thumbnails which aid in reinforcing the concept behind your content. Below are a few quick tips regarding the dimensions and designs

- The thumbnail size for YouTube is 1280 x 720 pixels.

- Save as BMP, GIF, PNG or JPG.

- Make efforts to use a ratio of 16:9. It is the most common for YouTube players.

- Ensure it is as appealing as possible with creative use of text, close-ups, and color.

- Don't forget that the thumbnail will seem little on mobile phones. Make sure all graphics and text are clearly visible.

- Let your resolution be as high as possible without exceeding the limit of 2MB.

- Brand your content using your own photo, logo and other elements of branding.

- You don't have to be a graphic designer to create custom thumbnails. With the help of online tools for design like Adobe Spark or Canva, your job will be easier.

### Engage with Your Viewers

It is essential that you do not forget that YouTube is a social media outlet, and therefore requires social interaction. If you just post videos without encouraging discussion and comments, you are not doing the right thing.

YouTube rewards channels that have lots of engagement. This also includes the overall watch time, comments, likes and dislikes and the total time spent on the channel. Make efforts to respond to all the comments you receive if you can. Also, ensure you request your users to engage with visual and audio prompts.

### *Get Branded*

So you have great content. But is your channel appealing visually? If you want viewers to be serious about your YouTube channel and subscribe, you need to have a more professional look. Branding your channel will also aid your users in recognizing your content instantly.

If you run a website or blog, you most likely have some kind of feel or look you utilize in distinguishing yourself from other companies or individuals. So it is only smart to move the branding to your channel on YouTube as well.

Asides from visual branding, you can add custom URLs to the header of your channel. Don't forget to write a great bio about what yourself and what your videos cover.

## Promote Your Video on Social Networking Websites

As long as you have not been living under a rock, you certainly know what social networking sites. Lots of individuals know about them these days. They are platforms where individuals that have common interests who have possibly never met physically gather.

YouTube is a form of social networking website because it aids in promoting communication through the internet among individuals with the same interest. Getting more subscribers and views on YouTube is not a complicated process. Although it may seem difficult to lots of individuals, if you know how to promote your YouTube channel on numerous social media platforms, you will see your subscriptions and views go drastically.

So we are going to be focusing on a few of the top options with the most traffic. How do you promote your channel on these websites?

## *Offer Your Audience A Reason to Follow Your Social Media Pages*

First, you have to offer your YouTube audience a reason to follow you on social media. This means you need to provide them with original content they will be unable to get from any other location. This means you need to ensure you do not post excessive repeat content across diverse social media outlets.

For example, individuals following you on Facebook may do so just to see behind-the-scenes videos from your next YouTube video. Don't just cross-post pictures and videos to Facebook or your audience won't see any need to follow you on the two networks.

Although it is appropriate to do a bit of cross-posting for viewers who are not following you on all your social media platforms, be sure you are posting original content on each. On Twitter, you could place a hint on what users can expect, on Facebook you could take opinion polls, on

Instagram, you could post behind the scene images and so on.

### Use Video Ads

Video ads let you promote your service, product or brand with the help of a video. You will be able to create a video ad using the manager. You will equally be able to boost a Facebook page post which comes with a video. Video ads will show up on Instagram, Facebook, and messenger.

### Facebook

Facebook lets you post various forms of items on your page. These range from pictures, to applications to videos. So you can attach your most recent videos on Facebook. There is equally another means of promoting your new videos using Facebook. All you have to do is select the Update Status button. It informs your friends about new videos.

For example, it writes: Just uploaded a YouTube video on how to train your dog". Every time you update your status, it notifies your friends anytime they log on.

## LinkedIn

This is another great site for networking that has a status feature. Regularly, LinkedIn notifies you about who is working on what and when two people connect.

If you mention your video in this context, you can quickly send a notification to people who have shown an interest in what you are doing and your work. The same applies to your WhatsApp status and Blackberry status, why not use those to promote your channel as well?

## Twitter

This is a website for social networking that lets you monitor the activities of your twitter followers via phone, instant messaging and Twitter website itself.

This is another way of interacting with your

audience. If individuals decide to follow you on Twitter, they will be able to get your tweets all-day. This way, they can actually feel connected to you.

You can equally create a Twitter chat related to your new YouTube video by planning a precise moment when you and your audience will be active and online on Twitter. Ensure you determine on the hashtag you would use for your Twitter chat. For example. The hashtag could be the name of your YouTube channel followed by chat. Then you can leave questions for your audience and inspire them to leave a response using your chat hashtag.

When you run a search on Twitter, you will see tweets linked with your chat showing up in real time. This is a great way to promote, interact and engage with your audience on a new level.

It is an excellent platform for promoting a new video, and lots of YouTubers use it. In fact, YouTube itself utilizes Twitter to offer its followers with tweets on YouTube happenings, news as well as featured videos.

### *Use Google+*

Google+ is rising in popularity each day. By developing a Google+ community, you will be able to provide your viewers with a productive space where they can speak about subjects that are significant to your YouTube channel and their interests. They will be able to make suggestions, post images, ask questions among others.

This way, you will be able to draw new subscribers from Google+ as well.

### *Reddit*

This is a website where users can submit links to videos, articles and other content on the web they find intriguing. Other members then take a vote on the submission offering them a thumbs down or thumbs up.

If you have a great video, it will get a lot of votes

and a large percentage of affirmative votes. Both of them will result in many more views. To begin, become a member of this site. If you are not a member yet, you will still be able to submit links to your videos. You will be asked for a description and title so ensure you place the best you can come up with.

You need to send them only your best videos as opposed to every video you produce. If you keep self-promoting yourself on this website, you can easily be noticed and severely criticized. But not to worry, the instant you show your audience the best videos in your arsenal, they will most likely go check out your past work.

### *Maintain a Tumblr Blog*

Tumblr is perhaps one of the undervalued social networks existing today. A lot of people utilize it, and it is ideal for sharing using its easy options for re-blogging.

This great platform gives you the opportunity to

share your videos alongside short-term blog posts to get more people sharing and viewing with friends. Asides from discussing your blogs more elaborately, you will be able to develop more significant content for your YouTube audience using Tumblr blog posts.

## Choose the Ideal Social Networks for Your Fans

With lots of social networks to select from, you may be wondering. "Do I need to be in every one of them? It is utterly dependent on you. However, you should research where all your viewers spend time online and place emphasis on those platforms specifically.

For example, beauty and makeup vloggers will be successful with networks that are image based like Instagram and Twitter. Twitter has a considerable portion of the tech world, so if you are a tech vlogger, your presence on Twitter has to be great. Everyone loves Facebook, so irrespective of what niche you are in on YouTube, you need to have a page on Facebook.

By using these promotion tips and employing proper practices for all your social media presences, you are bound to see drastic enhancement in your YouTube subscriptions and views.

### *Promoting Your YouTube Channel Via Your Blog*

You are likely utilizing a blog to draw in traffic from search engines. So, why not use it in promoting your YouTube videos as well.

It is not difficult to attach videos to a majority of the blogging platforms. All you have to do is to create a post dedicated to the video and add a description to it. You also can make a section for videos on your website.

If you plan on using this technique, below are a few tips:

- Boost clicks using a compelling headline.

- Describe or if possible, transcribe the video to produce content rich in keywords.

- Add call-to-action asking viewers to subscribe to your channel on YouTube.

- Include a video to a YouTube playlist adding significant keywords.

## *Try Being A Guest Contributor*

Guest blogging aids in showcasing your knowledge by offering amazing content to fans across your niche. You will be able to attach YouTube videos to follow the contribution or in the author bio, mention your YouTube channel.

Write content for blogs, websites, and magazine covering content in your field. After your contribution, leave a comment to pull in more crowd to your YouTube channel.

Do not undermine the local press as well. Newspapers in small towns are always in search of content, so find the name of the right editor and pitch your article. You could also search for Interview opportunities to help with promotion.

### *Using Podcasts*

Creating a podcast is a distinct method of drawing attention to your videos on YouTube. All you require is a computer, mic, and software for editing audio. You will be able to upload any podcast you produce on YouTube also. This will offer you much more content on your channel as well.

### *Use Internet Forums*

You can become a member of internet forums, most of which come with low or free membership fees. Then, you contribute to subjects that are in line with your YouTube videos. So if your videos focus on fitness, participate in fitness forums.

The trick here is to add your YouTube channel or Video URL in the forum signature. A line of text will show up underneath each post you make.

## *Promote Videos with The Help of Pop-Ups*

Try using pop-ups when you want to promote videos on your channel. Most pop-ups request for contact information, but this is not necessary. Pop-ups are ideal methods of promoting your videos on YouTube and urge sharing on social media.

Channel owners can utilize WisePops for embedding and playing videos on the pop-up. Target visitors by the browser, source, device or frequency. This is really helpful if you need to promote a video to a precise audience.

### *Share Your Videos Using Email*

When you manage an email effectively, it can be a potent tool for marketing. That is not all, and it costs less than advertising on social media.

So how do you go about this?

- Utilize features like merge tag to attach

screenshots of your video directly to your email. The screenshots will then have a link to the actual video.

- TailoredMail allows you to attach videos in your email campaigns. This service also aids in tracking video length, view counts, device breakdown and sharing behavior.

### *Show Up*

If you are operating your YouTube channel on your own or as part of a little company, it can be of great benefit to letting your face show on screen. Placing your face on a brand ensures your viewers can connect with ease to you as a person.

It is majorly crucial for business coaches, bloggers and fitness experts among others. You don't have to place your face in all the videos. However, it is essential that you personally reach out to your viewers after a few videos.

Also, if you are this kind of YouTuber, utilize a picture of yourself on your channel as opposed to your picture.

## *Advertise Your Channel*

Utilizing YouTube advertising can aid you in promoting your channel to specific groups of your viewers.

Below are some useful tips on ways you can pay to promote your channel using YouTube advertising:

- As opposed to longer ads, shorter ones have better rates of views. Aiming for 20-60 seconds for most kinds of video ads is ideal.

- First impressions are crucial. If there are lots of individual's rushing through your skippable ads, try to change the initial 5 seconds.

- Do not forget how crucial CTAs are. Clarify to the viewers what you need them to do next if you want them to share your content, check out your website, make a purchase or want them to subscribe.

- Utilizing TrueView inodisplay ads also known as video discovery ads can be an excellent method of promoting your current videos. Ensure you have a well-optimized content that aids in catering to the requirements of your viewers.

When you are good to go, you can begin running a campaign on Google AdWords to enhance your video marketing, seeping up the growth of your channel and ensuring more people can see your videos. The great news is that you will be able to create your budget. Pay for promoting videos on your channel and stick to the right costs for your company.

### *Run YouTube Contests and Giveaways*

If you want to promote your channel on YouTube in a creative and fun manner, a great giveaway is a route to take.

Contests and giveaways are amazing strategies for engaging your viewers. Everyone loves free stuff. Utilize prices as a motivation to get the audience to subscribe to your channel.

Request that your audience leave comments as they view. Call on your client to upload videos which show them utilizing your service or product.

There are numerous methods of running a prosperous contest on YouTube. Ascertain it follows all the guidelines and policies provided by YouTube. Next, promote the giveaway on your website, social media, and YouTube to spread the word.

If you do it correctly, a YouTube giveaway, asides from promoting your channel, can also aid in generating leads, attracting subscribers and creating a more enthusiastic and loyal community.

### *Enhance the Frequency of Your Uploads*

This may not seem easy initially, but to increase your viewers, you have to enhance the frequency at which you post videos to no less than one video every week. To don't need an expensive budget to do this. Smartphones today provide amazing tools and video recording capacity.

Being consistent is crucial. Make efforts to upload the same time every week or day based on your frequency. Also, ensure you keep your subscribers informed about when you would upload new videos and follow that schedule.

Do not forget that pushing engagement with quality content is what grows engaged followers. Be true to your brand and yourself and interact with your audience as you go on.

## How Can I Get Casual Viewers To Subscribe?

Has any of your friends shared with you a link on YouTube you fancied so much you subscribed to the channel on YouTube to ensure you see the next video? Well, lots of people do this. The issue is that because most of these videos which go viral are one-hit wonders, viewers hardly expect that the next one is going to be as entertaining.

Also, not many users know that YouTube has channels, so subscribing is not as natural as following or liking. So, how can you deal with these issues and get the best of your channel?

The steps below can help you.

### *Provide the Appropriate Content*

Studies have proven that shared and consumed are in the same group. Aside from categorization, your content must go with your brand.

In essence, you do not just develop content for the sake of sharing. Create it to fortify your brand. Also, make sure you clearly define the purpose and role of your content on YouTube.

YouTube differs from other outlets like Twitter,

Facebook or vine, so your approach and content has to reveal his understanding. Lastly, offer your audience a purpose to subscribe like advice or tips, product premieres or demos, ongoing original content among others.

### Develop Branded Channel Art

The most significant part of branding on the page of a channel is channel art. So, ensure you use this chance to display the personality of your brand. The design is scalable across any kind of device. It ensures viewers can enjoy the same entertaining, visually compelling and original brand experience anytime and anywhere. A more complete, branded YouTube channel page will aid viewers in connecting with your channel emotionally, which in turn can transform casual viewers into devoted subscribers.

### Have A Fascinating Trailer

YouTube's form of a CTA, which is the recent trailer feature is a fantastic chance for brands to transform audience to subscribers. It allows brands to pick videos to play only for viewers who have not subscribed.

The viewer falls on a brand channel, and without any prompt, the trailer video starts to play. Effectively utilize these tools, and it will encourage your audience to subscribe.

### Add A Call to Action

If you don't remind or ask them, then your audience won't remember or know they should subscribe.

For example, *"To get notifications when we post new videos, click on the SUBSCRIBE button below.*

### Partner with Other YouTube Video Creators

Every major YouTuber engages in this, and you can also. By collaborating with other creators, it exposes you to their viewers. Look for similar channels in your niche and contact them.

Ensure you choose channels that have a subscriber size similar to yours. If you have 30,000 subscribers, don't contact someone with 600,000.

### Develop Amazing Playlists

Do you have a group of videos that follow one another? Place them in a list together. It will motivate them to watch them all at once, and they will have a higher likelihood of subscribing to your channel because they will be able to see the video you upload next.

### Produce Searchable Titles

For many people, the last thing they come up with are the titles. For this reason, they do not put a lot of consideration when choosing them. However, this is a huge mistake.

Come up with a great title in advance and lots of people will locate your videos and equally subscribe to your channel.

# How Can I Collaborate With Other Creators?

### *Why should you collaborate?*

The idea of attaining new followers is what inspires lots of content creators to partner with one another. Working alongside another YouTuber is a fantastic way of introducing your channel to a new fan base entirely. If you properly select your collaborator, you will be targeting an audience base who should already have an interest in the kinds of videos you produce.

That is not all. Partnering with other YouTubers is a fantastic way to urge yourself to be more original by providing you with new content concepts. However, partnering with other YouTubers does a whole lot more than increasing your creativity. They aid you in establishing a significant association with people who are relevant within your niche, and this capacity to network can be quite beneficial.

Asides from attaining a new audience, collaborations provide you with access to individuals that can be of use to you later. These are people who can be your industry partners, mentors among a host of others.

Collaborations open you to a world of opportunities you may not have gotten access to if you refuse to work with other YouTubers.

## How to Launch A YouTube Collaboration Which Is Successful?

To a person who is new on YouTube, the concept of collaboration with others could be scary. It is normal for you to be a little skeptical initially, but the instant you begin, you will understand that the process is quicker than you thought at first.

Breaking the process down into numerous actionable steps will aid in making collaborating seem more attainable in your head. The steps

below will assist you in working with other YouTubers.

They are:

## *Locating the Proper Individuals to Collaborate With*

There are numerous YouTubers available today, so it should not be so tedious to find the right individual to work with. This is so long as you can go past the noise and locate the right individuals.

Google has a community which is dedicated to prospective partners on YouTube. Go through the numerous profiles and posts to find out which of the community members has what you need in a collaborator.

## *Become a member of numerous forums online*

There are a host of forums that can aid you in locating your next collaborator. These kinds of online forums are filled with members who are always active. In essence, it should not be difficult to find someone you can work with.

From this moment, you need to put down a list of possible collaborators alongside their contact information. This will let you go through each of them one after the other when you are ready to contact them.

### *Make Contact*

The instant you are satisfied with your list of possible collaborators, you can start to make contact one after the other.

The best method of reaching out to a possible collaborator is using social media or email. A YouTuber that has the desire to collaborate with others, irrespective of if it is fellow creators of contents or brands, needs to have listed their business email on their channels alongside their handles on social media.

Send an elaborate proposal to the contact emails you can locate. Ensure you add a little information about your channel, the kind of videos you create and how the collaboration can benefit you both.

If you are unable to locate a contact email on their profile on YouTube, make efforts to reach out to them via their other accounts on social media.

### *Producing Collab Videos*

After you have sent some proposals to a range of YouTubers, you are certainly going to get some responses.

One someone accepts to collaborate with you, and you can start to work on your video ideas. You can get your inspiration from YouTube to help give you creative ideas.

Nowadays, it is not necessary for you to be in the same location as your collaborator to make a collab video. A popular Story Time YouTuber, Nikki Glamour collaborates with other video creators on YouTube in the beauty and lifestyle niche frequently.

They usually format a layout where they produce videos relating to similar events that occurred in their lives. Then, they direct their audience to view the video of one another. Nikki tells her story in a video, while Trinity Jae, her collaborator explains it from her point of view in her video.

But obviously, appearing on the video of one another is the best method of collaborating with another YouTuber.

Shane Dawson and Miranda Sings, who are both lifestyle and comedy content creators, offered their subscribers something to look forward to as regards appearing in the video of one another.

Their collab video- Trying Mexican Candles, attained more than 9 million views since it got uploaded. This just proves the amount of power a collab video can offer.

## *Sharing*

Your YouTube collaboration does not end after uploading the video. Once you are through uploading on your individual channels, you both have to go further by engaging in a shared campaign.

Your initial collab video is a core one, and it is only necessary that you provide it with the necessary promotion. In sharing your video, you will be able to reach out into lots more viewers and attract them to your channel. Lots of viewers enjoy collab videos, and they would be keen on checking out your content even if they know nothing about you.

## *Retention of Viewers*

Now that all these viewers have subscribed, the next trial will be to ensure they remain subscribed for as long as they can. Use the lessons from your collaborators and provide your recent subscribers with lots of additional reasons to always open your channel.

You need to do all you can to transform your new subscribers into loyal fans. You need to also ensure you stay in contact with your collaborator. Drop by frequently so it won't be difficult contacting them later on.

## Two Heads Are Better Than One

The greatest asset YouTube has are its numerous content creators. Without these YouTubers creating videos every other second, YouTube would not be as popular as it is today.

You fellow content creators can also be a valuable asset to you if you take the step and start collaborating. Collaborating with individuals having more subscribers than you may seem quite scary at first, but if you don't take action, you will never know what a possible collaboration can do for your channel.

Utilize collaborations as a chance to find new concepts and video formats that will aid in enhancing your channel. Partnerships can also assist you in penetrating an untapped viewership you may not have come across by yourself.

Never undermine the strength of a great collaboration. Collaborating with the appropriate content creator may be just the thing you require to make your channel successful.

## How Can I Make Clickable Thumbnails?

Are you thinking of how to make great thumbnails? Then read on. When you are developing content and uploading YouTube videos, the thumbnail may not seem like a crucial aspect of your video. You may think that, so long as you have great content, your thumbnail isn't a problem.

This is not true. An excellent thumbnail is what your viewers see first when going through YouTube. It is basically your video's first impression, and it basically determines if they would click or not. Creating a professional

YouTube thumbnail, asides from helping you enhance the brand of your channel, also draw in more eyes and visitors to your content.

So how can you create effective thumbnails? Below are a few steps that can help you begin:

### *Utilize the Appropriate Thumbnail Dimensions For YouTube*

If you would take the time to create a thumbnail that has a professional look, you need to ensure you are utilizing the proper dimensions and sizing.

Using YouTube guidelines, you should have a thumbnail image of 1280 x 720 pixels with the least width of 640 pixels. A 16:9 ratio works best as most YouTube previews and players use it.

It's a huge mistake to make a thumbnail image that is too little. Even though thumbnail images appear quite small in the YouTube search result, also remember that it is equally possible to embed YouTube videos. Due to this, it's best to go with a larger image size will be scaled down as opposed to a little size which will be scaled up.

## *Add a Title to Your Thumbnails On YouTube*

There are numerous benefits you gain when you add text heading on the thumbnail of your videos. The major one is that it provides the viewers with more perspective into your video. There are lots of videos with numbered text headings in the thumbnail. Similar to TV shows with numbered seasons and episodes, numbering your thumbnails will aid your audience in keeping up with the content they are viewing.

Brands like Apple add text headings in their thumbnails to offer an extra perspective that is not instantly obvious.

## *Utilize Good Contrast in Your Thumbnail Design*

Adding a title to your thumbnail is crucial. However, if you are unable to read it, then what is the essence. This is where contrast is useful. While there are a host of diverse kinds of contrast, the most crucial one to put into consideration is color contrast.

If two colors are distinct from one another like white and red, they have high contrast. On the other hand, if they look like one another like orange and red, then they have low contrast.

When creating an image for your thumbnail, always ensure that your text nicely contrasts with your background. If needed, you can utilize tools like Adobe Color to ensure that your colors effectively contrast.

### *Be Consistent with The Font and Design of Your YouTube Thumbnail*

It is always crucial to get your viewers familiar with your content and brand. An excellent method of doing this is to ensure your thumbnails remain consistent using the same memorable colors, style front, and great design.

To start, take a professional image yourself or select one from a stock image website. After getting this professional image, you can then include a text heading above the image using a font style that signifies your style. If you are not good at using Photoshop, you can utilize Snappa for creating free YouTube thumbnails.

## *Use Pictures That Grab Attention in Your YouTube Thumbnails*

Powerful visuals are crucial in catching your viewers' attention. An image of high-quality which functions as a video teaser will once again provide context. However, it is also an excellent chance for your viewers to get familiar with you.

## *Be Accurate and Honest in Your Thumbnails*

It is possible to use click bait to get users to check out your videos by misleading them with headlines and thumbnails. This will damage your reputation and brand. Asides that, YouTube will prevent your videos from coming up in search results if you have excessively high bounce rates.

The thumbnail aims to provide context, so adding an image that does not show what your video contains will cause more harm than benefit. Look for the most crucial part or point of your video and develop your thumbnail based on that.

Let your thumbnail act as your video teaser without showing too much. Display enough to ensure users click and view what you have to provide or say.

The significance of thumbnails on YouTube cannot be overemphasized. Asides from making a considerable impact as regards click-through rates, it also plays a crucial role in branding your channel.

# Conclusion

YouTube has shown us how powerful online videos can be. It has also given the average individual the chance to get a broad platform for saying what he or she feels. It has also offered owners of business a very great tool for marketing themselves and business.

It is only ideal that you take advantage of what YouTube offers as it would only keep growing with time. The competition for viewership online is fierce and breaking in may not be easy. If you are trying to break into the industry and build yourself as a video creator, you certainly have a lot to do to stand out.

But without a doubt, there is a massive opportunity in this platform as it has helped create numerous generations of stars on YouTube. To be successful on YouTube, you need to know the things that work and things that don't.

Above, I have offered you a lot of information you can read and implement to make your start easier than usual. Now, it is left to you to begin and come up with your original technique to draw in a loyal fan base and subscribers.

So why wait? Take the step now.